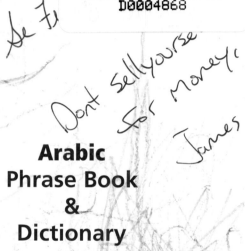

Arabic
Phrase Book
&
Dictionary

Don't sell yourse
for money,
James

First thing, learn: "I don't speak
← Arabic" in Arabic!
~ Candon

Berlitz Publishing
New York   Munich   Singapore

Contacting the Editors
Every effort has been made to provide accurate information in this publication, but changes are inevitable. The publisher cannot be responsible for any resulting loss, inconvenience or injury. We would appreciate it if readers would call our attention to any errors or outdated information. We also welcome your suggestions; if you come across a relevant expression not in our phrase book, please contact us: Berlitz Publishing, 193 Morris Avenue, Springfield, NJ 07081, USA, email: comments@berlitzbooks.com

Fifth Printing: April 2009
Printed in Singapore

Publishing Director: Sheryl Olinsky Borg
Senior Editor/Project Manager: Lorraine Sova
Translation: Lexus Ltd with Alex Chapman
Cover Design: Claudia Petrilli
Interior Design: Derrick Lim, Juergen Bartz
Production Manager: Elizabeth Gaynor
Cover Photo: Punchstock
Interior Photos: p. 12, ©Studio Fourteen/BrandX/Age Fotostock; p.15, ©Paul Cowan, 2006/Shutterstock, Inc.; p. 17, ©Kevin Phillips; p. 27, ©Iconotec/Fotosearch.com; p. 37, ©Albo, 2006/Shutterstock, Inc.; p. 36, ©Adrian Lindley/Shutterstock, Inc.; p. 36, ©Louise Batalla Duran/wandering-spirit-travel-images; p. 39, ©Ron Hayes/Alamy; p. 51, ©Paul Cowan, 2006/Shutterstock, Inc.; p. 53, ©Udo Kroener/Alamy; p. 58, ©Jean-Blaise Hall/Photo Alto/Jupiter Images; p. 61, ©Mark Phillips/Alamy; p. 72, ©Dan Peretz, 2006/Shutterstock, Inc.; p. 80, ©www.copix.co.us; p. 84, ©J.D. Dallet/arabianEye/Redux; p. 98, ©Michele Falzone; p. 101, ©Digital Vision/Fotosearch.com; p. 106, ©Digital Vision/Fotosearch.com; p. 108, ©Digital Vision/Fotosearch.com; p. 111, ©Jim Zuckerman/Corbis; p. 116, ©Digital Vision/Fotosearch.com; p. 123, ©Martin Child/Digital Vision/Getty Images; p. 133, ©Insy Shah/Gulfimages; p. 139, ©John Wreford; p. 140, ©Royalty-Free/Corbis; p. 142, ©Digital Vision/Fotosearch.com; p. 144, ©Liz Boyd/Alamy; p. 148, ©David McKee, 2006/Shutterstock, Inc.; p. 149, ©Izzet Keribar/Images&Stories; p. 151, ©Nikolai Ignatiev/arabianEye/Redux; p. 159, ©Udo Kroener/Alamy; p. 171, ©Pankaj & Insy Shah/Gulfimages

[Handwritten note:] Enjoy Qatar & the 3 beers a day you can have!! Kristine

Contents

Survival

Food

People

Fun

Special Needs

Resources

Dictionary

Pronunciation

This section is designed to make you familiar with the sounds of Arabic using our simplified phonetic transcription. You'll find the pronunciation of the Arabic letters and sounds explained below, together with their "imitated" equivalents. This system is used throughout the phrase book; simply read the pronunciation as if it were English, noting any special rules below.

Consonants

Letter	Approximate Pronunciation	Symbol	Example	Pronunciation
ب	b as in bat	b	بنت	bint
ت	t as in tin	t	تكييف	takyeef
ث	t as in tin[1]	t	ثلاجة	tallaaja
ج	j as in jam[2]	j	جميل	jameel
ح	strong, breathy h	H	صحون	suHoon
خ	h from back of throat as in Scottish loch	kh	خدمة	khedma
د	d as in dad	d	درج	daraj
ذ	z as in zebra[3]	z	هذا	haaza
ر	r as in rain	r	رجل	rajul
ز	z as in zebra	z	زيت	zayt
س	s as in sun	s	سلام	salaam
ش	sh as in shut	sh	شمس	shams
ص	strong, emphatic s	s	صباح	sabaaH
ض	strong, emphatic d	d	اضافى	edaafee

[1] Can be pronounced th as in thin in formal language.
[2] In Egyptian Arabic this may also be pronounced as g in gate.
[3] Can be pronounced th as in that in formal language.

Letter	Approximate Pronunciation	Symbol	Example	Pronunciation
ط	strong, emphatic t	t	بطاقة	bi<u>t</u>aaqa
ظ	strong, emphatic z	z	إنتظار	inti<u>z</u>aar
ع	as the a in a strongly pronounced apple; the apostrophe shows a sharp start to the word or syllable	'aa	عندي	<u>'aa</u>ndee
غ	a softer form of kh, as in loch, but gently holding the sound	gh	غرفة	<u>gh</u>urfa
ف	like f in fan	f	فرن	furn
ق	q pronounced from back of throat (sometimes dropped in spoken Arabic)	q	قريب	<u>q</u>areeb
ك	k as in kite	k	كيف	kayf
ل	l as in lip	l	لماذا	<u>l</u>imaaza
م	m as in man	m	ممسحة	<u>m</u>i<u>m</u>saHa
ن	n as in never	n	نور	noor
ه	h as in hat	h	هنا	<u>h</u>una
ؤ	w as in win	w	وسط	wast
ي	y as in yet	y	يمين	<u>y</u>a<u>m</u>een
ء	the apostrophe shows a sharp start to the word or syllable and is generally omitted in writing where the sound occurs naturally at the beginning of a word	'	تدفئة	tadf<u>i</u>'a

Short Vowels

Letter	Approximate Pronunciation	Symbol	Example	Pronunciation
ـَ	a as in bat	a	لَمبَة	lamba
ـُ	u as in but	u	گُل	kul
ـِ	i as in bit	i	بِنت	bint

Long Vowels

Letter	Approximate Pronunciation	Symbol	Example	Pronunciation
آ	ar as in dark	aa	هنَاك	hun<u>aak</u>
وُ	oo as in boot	oo	فطوُر	fut<u>oor</u>
ى	ee as in meet	ee	تكِييف	tak<u>yeef</u>
و	o as in home	oh	يوُم	y<u>oh</u>m
ـَى	ay as in say	ay	إثنَين	itn<u>ayn</u>

Vowels take the form of diacritics when they are short vowels but come attached to a particular consonant when they are long.

i Arabic is written right to left (except for numbers). Most Arabic letters change their form slightly, depending on whether they are at the beginning, in the middle or at the end of a word. The Arabic letters in the chart above are shown in their basic stand-alone position.

Arabic is a gender-specific language; nouns are masculine or feminine. Verb forms may change based on whether the person spoken to is male or female. For simplicity, only forms used to address a man have been included, except where indicated. For female form, see page 106.

Spoken Arabic varies from country to country. The Arabic used in this book is known as Modern Standard Arabic. It is used in the Arab media and will be understood in all Arabic-speaking countries.

How to Use This Book

These essential phrases can also be heard on the audio CD.

Sometimes you see two alternatives in italics, separated by a slash. Choose the one that's right for your situation.

Essential

I'm on *vacation [holiday]/business.*	أنا في إجازة/في رحلة عمل. <u>ana</u> fee e<u>jaa</u>za/fee ri<u>H</u>lat '<u>aa</u>mal
I'm going to…	أنا ذاهب♂/ذاهبة♀ إلى… <u>ana</u> <u>zaa</u>hib♂/ <u>zaa</u>hiba♀ ila…
I'm staying at the… Hotel.	أنا نازل♂/نازلة♀ في فندق… ana <u>naa</u>zil♂/ <u>naa</u>zila♀ fee <u>fun</u>duq…

You May See…

الجمرك al-<u>jum</u>ruk	customs
بضائع معفية من الضرائب bi<u>daa</u>i'aa mo'a<u>fee</u>ya min al-da<u>raa</u>'ib	duty-free goods

ATM, Bank and Currency Exchange

My card…	بطاقتي… bi<u>taa</u>qatee…
– was lost	ضاعت <u>daa</u>'at
– was stolen	سرقت <u>su</u>riqat
– doesn't work	لا تعمل laa <u>ta</u>'aamal

Any of the words or phrases preceded by dashes can be plugged into the sentence above.

Words you may see are shown in *You May See* boxes.

Arabic language phrases appear in red.

Read the simplified pronunciation as if it were English. For more on pronunciation, see page 7.

Work and School

I...   ...أنا _a_na...

– am a consultant   مستشار♂/مستشارة♀   musta<u>shaar</u>♂/
                                                 musta<u>shaa</u>ra ♀

– am unemployed   غير موظف♂/غير موظفة♀   <u>ghayr</u>
                                                 mu<u>wazz</u>af/ ♀ gha

When different gender forms apply, the masculine form is followed by ♂; feminine by ♀.

– work at home   أعمل في البيت

▶For business travel, see page 141.

The arrow indicates a cross reference where you'll find related phrases.

Information boxes contain relevant country, culture and language tips.

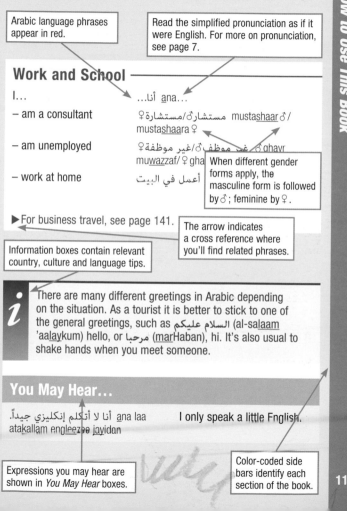

i There are many different greetings in Arabic depending on the situation. As a tourist it is better to stick to one of the general greetings, such as السلام عليكم (al-sa<u>laam</u> 'aa<u>lay</u>kum) hello, or مرحبا (<u>mar</u>Haban), hi. It's also usual to shake hands when you meet someone.

You May Hear...

أنا لا أتكلم إنكليزي جيداً. _a_na laa   I only speak a little English.
ata<u>kall</u>am eng<u>leez</u>ee <u>jay</u>idan

Expressions you may hear are shown in *You May Hear* boxes.

Color-coded side bars identify each section of the book.

11

▼ Survival

Arrival and Departure

Essential

I'm on *vacation* [holiday]/*business*.	أنا في إجازة/في رحلة عمل. <u>a</u>na fee ejaaza/fee ri<u>H</u>lat 'aa<u>m</u>al
I'm going to…	أنا ذاهب♂/ذاهبة♀ إلى… <u>a</u>na z<u>aa</u>hib♂ / z<u>aa</u>hiba♀ ila…
I'm staying at the… Hotel.	أنا نازل♂/نازلة♀ في فندق… ana n<u>aa</u>zil♂ / n<u>aa</u>zila♀ fee f<u>u</u>nduq…

You May Hear…

جواز سفرك من فضلك. jaw<u>aa</u>z <u>s</u>afrak min <u>fad</u>lak	Your passport, please.
ما الغرض من زيارتك؟ maa al-ghard min ziy<u>aa</u>ratak	What's the purpose of your visit?
أين ستنزل؟ ayn sa-t<u>a</u>nzil	Where are you staying?
كم ستستغرق زيارتك؟ kam sa'tast<u>a</u>ghriq ziy<u>aa</u>ratak	How long are you staying?
من يرافقك؟ man yur<u>aa</u>fiqak	Who are you here with?

Passport Control and Customs

I'm just passing through.	أنا هنا في مرور. <u>a</u>na h<u>u</u>na fee mur<u>oo</u>r
I'd like to declare…	أريد الإعلان عن… oor<u>ee</u>d al-e'aal<u>aa</u>n 'aan…
I have nothing to declare.	ليس عندي أي شيء للإعلان عنه. laysa 'aandee ay shay lil-e'aal<u>aa</u>n 'aanhu

You May Hear...

هل عندك أي شيء للإعلان عنه؟ hal 'aandak ay shay lil- e'aalaan 'aanhu	Anything to declare?
يجب دفع رسوم على هذا. yajib dafa' rusoom ala haza	You must pay duty on this.
افتح هذه الحقيبة. eftaH hazih al-Haqeeba	Open this bag.

You May See...

الجمرك al-jumruk	customs
بضائع معفية من الضرائب bidaai'aa mo'aafeeya min al-daraa'ib	duty-free goods
بضائع للإعلان عنها bidaai'aa lil-e'aalaan 'aanha	goods to declare
لا شيء للإعلان عنه laa shay lil-e'aalaan 'aanhu	nothing to declare
مراقبة جوازات السفر muraaqabat jawazaat al-safar	passport control
الشرطة al-shurta	police

i Visas are needed to enter most Middle Eastern countries. Sometimes they can be bought at the point of entry, but you will need to check with your travel agent or consulate as this varies from country to country and from year to year. Usually it is better to obtain your visa in your own country prior to travel.

Money and Banking

Essential

Where's…?	أين...؟ ...ayn
– the ATM	الصراف الآلي al-saraaf al-'aalee
– the bank	البنك al-bank
– the currency exchange office	مكتب تبديل العملات maktab tabdeel al-'umlaat
When does the bank *open/close*?	متى يفتح/يغلق البنك؟ mata yaftaH/yaghliq al-bank
I'd like to change *dollars/pounds* into…	أريد تبديل دولارات/ جنيهات إسترلينية إلى... ooreed tabdeel doolaaraat/jinayhaat esterleeneeya ila…
I'd like to cash traveler's checks [cheques].	أريد أن أصرف شيكات سياحية. ooreed an asrif sheekaat seeyaHeeya

ATM, Bank and Currency Exchange

I'd like to *change money/get a cash advance*.   أريد تبديل عملة/الحصول على دفعة مسبقة. ooreed tabdeel 'umla/al-husool 'ala duf'aa musabbaqa

What's the exchange *rate/fee*?   ما هو سعر/رسم الصرف؟ maa huwa si'r/rasm al-sarf

I think there's a mistake.   أعتقد أن هناك خطأ. a'aataqid an hunaak khata'

I lost my traveler's checks [cheques].   فقدت شيكاتي السياحية. faqadtu sheekaatee al-seeyaHeeya

My card…   بطاقتي… bitaaqatee…

– was lost   ضاعت daa'at

– was stolen   سرقت suriqat

– doesn't work   لا تعمل laa ta'aamal

The ATM ate my card.   الصراف الآلي سحب بطاقتي. al-saraaf al-'aalee saHab bitaaqatee

▶ For bank and credit cards, see page 121.

▶ For numbers, see page 168.

Cash can be obtained from ATMs (cash machines) with Visa, Eurocard, American Express and many other international cards. Instructions are often given in English. You can also change money at travel agencies and hotels, but the rate will not be as good. Remember your passport when you want to change money.

You May See…

أدخل بطاقتك هنا	<u>a</u>dkhil bi<u>taa</u>qatak <u>hu</u>na	insert card here
إلغاء	el<u>ghaa</u>'	cancel
تراجع	ta<u>raa</u>joo'	clear
أدخل	<u>a</u>dkhil	enter
الرقم السري	al-raqm al-<u>si</u>ree	PIN
سحب	<u>sa</u>Hab	withdrawal
من الحساب الجاري	min al-Hi<u>saab</u> al-<u>jaa</u>ree	from checking account
من حساب المدخرات	min Hi<u>saab</u> al-mudakha<u>raat</u>	from savings account
إيصال	ee<u>saal</u>	receipt

i

Currency types in the Arabic speaking region include:

dinar دينار (dee<u>naar</u>)   Algeria, Bahrain, Iraq, Jordan, Libya,
                                    Kuwait, Tunisia
pound جنيه (gu<u>nay</u>)   Egypt, Sudan
pound ليرة (<u>lee</u>ra)   Lebanon, Syria
dirham درهم (<u>dir</u>ham)   Morocco, United Arab Emirates
riyal ريال (ree<u>yaal</u>)   Oman, Qatar, Saudi Arabia, Yemen

Note: Although the currency in different countries may have
the same name, the value may vary enormously.

Transportation

Essential

How do I get to town?	كيف أصل إلى المدينة؟ kayf <u>a</u>sil <u>i</u>lal-ma<u>dee</u>na
Where's…?	أين...؟ ayn...
– the airport	المطار al-ma<u>taar</u>
– the train [railway] station	محطة القطار ma<u>Ha</u>tat al-qi<u>taar</u>
– the bus station	محطة الباص ma<u>Ha</u>tat al-baas
– the subway [underground] station	محطة مترو الأنفاق ma<u>Ha</u>tat <u>met</u>ro al-an<u>faaq</u>
How far is it?	كم هي بعيدة؟ kam <u>hi</u>ya ba'<u>ee</u>da
Where do I buy a ticket?	أين أشتري تذكرة؟ ayn ash<u>ta</u>ree <u>taz</u>kara
A *one-way/round-trip [return]* ticket to…	تذكرة ذهاب/ذهاب و عودة إلى... <u>taz</u>kara *ze<u>haab</u>/ze<u>haab</u> wa-'<u>oh</u>da* <u>i</u>la…
How much?	بكم؟ bi-<u>kam</u>

Which…?	؟...أي ay…
– gate	بوابة ba<u>waa</u>ba
– line	خـط khat
– platform	رصيف ra<u>seef</u>
Where can I get a taxi?	أين آخذ تاكسي؟ ayn '<u>a</u>khud <u>tak</u>see
Take me to this address.	أوصلني إلى هذا العنوان. oh<u>sil</u>nee <u>i</u>la <u>ha</u>za al-'un<u>waan</u>
Can I have a map?	ممكن خـريطة؟ <u>mum</u>kin kha<u>ree</u>ta

Ticketing

When's the…to Cairo?	متى موعد الـ...إلى القاهرة؟ <u>ma</u>ta <u>moh</u>'id al-...<u>i</u>lal-<u>qaa</u>hira
– (first) bus	(أول) باص (<u>a</u>wal) baas
– (next) flight	الرحلة الجوية (التالية) al-<u>ri</u>Hla al-<u>joh</u>weeya (al-taa<u>lee</u>ya)
– (last) train	القطار (الأخير) al-qi<u>taar</u> (al-a<u>kheer</u>)
Where do I buy a ticket?	أين أشتري تذكرة؟ ayn ash<u>ta</u>ree <u>taz</u>kara
One/two ticket(s), please.	تذكرة/تذكرتين، من فضلك. <u>taz</u>kara/ tazka<u>ra</u>tayn min <u>fad</u>lak
For…	لـ... li…
– today	اليوم al-<u>yohm</u>
– tonight	الليلة al-<u>lay</u>la
– tomorrow	غداً <u>gha</u>dan

▶ For days, see page 171.

▶ For time, see page 170.

A...ticket.	تذكرة... tazkara...
– one-way	ذهاب zehaab
– round-trip [return]	ذهاب وعـودة zehaab wa-ohda
– first class	درجة أولى daraja oola
– business class	درجة الأعمال darajat al-a'amaal
– economy class	درجة سياحية daraja siyaHeeya
How much?	بكم؟ bi-kam
Is there...discount?	هل هناك تخفيض...؟ hal hunaak takhfeed...
– a child	للأطفال lil-atfaal
– a student	للطلاب lil-tulaab
– a senior citizen	للمسنين lil-musineen
– a tourist	للسياح lil-sayaH
The (express/local) *train/bus*, please.	القطار/الباص (السريع/المحلي)، من فضلك. al-qitaar/al-baas (al-saree'a/al-maHalee) min fadlak
I have an e-ticket.	عندي تذكرة الكترونية. 'aandee tazkara elektroneeya
Can I buy a ticket on the *bus/train*?	ممكن أشتري تذكرة داخل الباص/القطار؟ mumkin ashtaree tazkara daakhil al-baas/al-qitaar
Do I have to stamp the ticket before boarding?	هل علي أن أختم التذكرة قبل الركوب؟ hal alaay an akhtum al-tazkara qabl al-rukoob
How long is this ticket valid?	ما طول صلاحية هـذه التذكرة؟ maa tool salaHeeya hazih al-tazkara
Can I return on the same ticket?	ممكن أن أعود عـلى نفس التذكرة؟ mumkin an a'ood ala nafs al-tazkara
I'd like to...my reservation.	أريد أن...حجزي. ooreed an...Hajzi
– cancel	ألغي 'alghi
– change	أغيـّر ooghayer
– confirm	أؤكـد oo'akid

Plane

Getting to the Airport

How much is a taxi to the airport?	بكم التاكسي إلى المطار؟ bi-kam al-<u>tak</u>see <u>i</u>lal-mataar
To…Airport, please.	إلى مطار…، من فضلك. <u>i</u>la-mataar… min <u>fad</u>lak
My airline is…	رحلتي على خطوط… ri<u>H</u>latee <u>a</u>la khutoot…
My flight leaves at…	رحلتي تقلع الساعة… ri<u>H</u>latee tuqla' al-<u>saa</u>'a…
I'm in a rush.	أنا مستعجل♂/أنا مستعجلة♀. <u>a</u>na musta'ajil♂ / <u>a</u>na musta'ajila♀

▶ For time, see page 170.

Can you take an alternate route?	ممكن تآخـذ طريق آخـر؟ <u>mum</u>kin <u>taa</u>khud tareeq <u>aa</u>khar
Can you drive *faster/ slower*?	ممكن تقـود السيارة بسرعة أكبر/بتمهـل أكثر؟ <u>mum</u>kin taqood al-sayaara *bi-<u>sur</u>'a <u>ak</u>bar/ bi-tama<u>hul</u> <u>ak</u>tar*

You May Hear…

ما هي الخطوط التي تسافرعـليها؟ maa <u>hiya</u> al-khutoot alatee tu<u>saa</u>fir <u>a</u>layha	What airline are you flying?
محلية أو دولية؟ ma<u>Haleeya</u> o doo<u>waleeya</u>	Domestic or international?
أي صالة؟ ay <u>saa</u>la	What terminal?

You May See…

قدوم qu<u>doom</u>	arrivals
مغادرة mu<u>ghaa</u>dara	departures
استلام الحقائب isti<u>laam</u> al-Haqaa'ib	baggage claim
الأمن al-amn	security

الرحلات الدولية al-riHlaat al-doowaleeya	international flights
الرحلات الداخلية al-riHlaat al-daakhileeya	domestic flights
إجراءات السفر ejra'aat al-safar	check-in
إجراءات السفر للتذاكر الالكترونية ejra'aat al-safar lil-tazaakir al-elektroneeya	e-ticket check-in
بوابات السفر bawabaat al-safar	departure gates

Check-in and Boarding

Where's check-in?	أين كاونتر إجراءات السفر؟ ayn kownter ijra'aat al-safar
My name is…	اسمي… ismee…
I'm going to…	أنا ذاهب إلى… ana zaahib ila…
I have…	معي… ma'ee…
– one suitcase	حقيبة واحدة Haqeeba waaHida
– two suitcases	حقيبتان Haqeebataan
– one carry-on [piece of hand luggage]	حقيبة يد واحدة Haqeebat yad waaHida
How much luggage is allowed?	كم من الأمتعة مسموح به؟ kam min al-amtia masmooH bih
Is that pounds or kilos?	هل هذا بالرطل أو بالكيلو؟ hal haza bil-rutl o bil-kilo
Which *terminal/gate*?	أي صالة/بوابة؟ ay saala/bawaaba
I'd like *a window/an aisle* seat.	أريد مقعد على النافذة/الممشى. ooreed maq'ad alal-naafiza/mamsha
When do we *leave/ arrive*?	متى نغادر/نصل؟ mata nooghaader/ nasil
Is the flight delayed?	هل الرحلة متأخرة؟ hal al-riHla muta'akhira
How late?	كم متأخرة؟ kam muta'akhira

22

You May Hear...

من التالي؟ man al-<u>taa</u>lee	Next!
جواز سفرك/تذكرتك، من فضلك. *jawaaz <u>saf</u>rak/<u>taz</u>karatak min <u>fad</u>lak*	Your *passport/ticket*, please.
هل ستودع أي أمتعة؟ hal sa-tu<u>wa</u>di' ay <u>am</u>ti'a	Are you checking any luggage?
هذا أكبر من حجم حقيبة اليد المسموح به. <u>haza akbar</u> min hajm Ha<u>qee</u>bat al-yad al-mas<u>mooH</u> bih	That's too large for a carry-on [to carry on board].
هل عبأت الحقائب بنفسك؟ hal <u>aba</u>'ata al-Ha<u>qaa</u>'ib bi-<u>naf</u>sak	Did you pack these bags yourself?
أفرغ جيوبك. '<u>af</u>ragh ju<u>yoo</u>bak	Empty your pockets.
إخلع حذائك. <u>ikhla</u>' Ha<u>zaa</u>'ik	Take off your shoes.
بدأ الآن صعود الركاب إلى الطائرة... <u>bada</u>' al-aan su<u>'ood</u> al-ru<u>kaab</u> <u>i</u>lal-<u>taa</u>'ira....	Now boarding...

Luggage

Where *is/are*...?	أين...؟ ayn...
– the luggage carts [trolleys]	عربات الأمتعة ara<u>baat</u> al-<u>am</u>ti'a
– the luggage lockers	خـزائن الأمتعة kha<u>zaa</u>'in al-<u>am</u>ti'a
– the baggage claim	استلام الأمتعة isti<u>laam</u> al-<u>am</u>ti'a
My luggage has been *lost/stolen*.	أمتعتي فقدت/سرقت. <u>am</u>ti'atee *fukadat/suraqat*
My suitcase is damaged.	حقيبتي تالفة. Ha<u>qee</u>batee <u>taa</u>lifa

Finding Your Way

Where *is/are*...?	أين...؟ ayn...
– the currency exchange	تبديل العملات tabdeel al-'umlaat
– the car rental [hire]	تأجير السيارات ta'ajeer al-sayaraat
– the exit	المخرج al-makhraj
– the taxis	التكاسي al-taksee
Is there...into town?	هل هناك...إلى المدينة؟ hal hunaak ...ilal-madeena
– a bus	باص baas
– a train	القطار qitaar
– a subway [underground]	مترو الأنفاق metro al-anfaaq

▶ For directions, see page 18.

Train

Where's the train [railway] station?	أين محطة القطار؟ ayn maHatat al-qitaar
How far is it?	كم هي بعيدة؟ kam hiya ba'eeda
Where *is/are*...?	أين...؟ ayn...
– the ticket office	مكتب التذاكر maktab al-tazaakir
– the information desk	الاستعلامات al-este'alaamaat
– the luggage lockers	خزائن الأمتعة khazaa'in al-amti'a
– the platforms	الأرصفة al-arsifa

▶ For directions, see page 34.
▶ For ticketing, see page 19.

You May See...

أرصفة arsifa	platforms
معلومات ma'aloomaat	information

حجوزات Hajoo<u>zaat</u>	reservations
غرفة انتظار <u>ghur</u>fat inti<u>zaar</u>	waiting room
قدوم qu<u>doom</u>	arrivals
مغادرة mo<u>ghaa</u>dira	departures

Questions

Is it a direct train?	هل هناك قطار مباشر؟ hal hu<u>naak</u> qi<u>taar</u> mu<u>baa</u>shir
Do I have to change trains?	هل علي أن أغيّر القطار؟ hal a<u>lay</u> an oo<u>ghay</u>er al-qi<u>taar</u>
Can I have a schedule [timetable]?	ممكن آخذ جدول مواعيد الرحلات؟ <u>mum</u>kin akhz <u>jad</u>wal mawaa'<u>eed</u> al-ri<u>H</u>laat
How long is the trip?	كم طول الرحلة؟ kam tool al-<u>riH</u>la
Is the train on time?	هل القطار في موعده؟ hal al-qi<u>taar</u> fee <u>moh</u>'idih

> *i*
> There are virtually no international Middle Eastern train services in operation, a notable exception being the Amman to Damascus route (part of the famous Ottoman Hijaaz train line). In some tourist areas, there are services running between cities, such as the Cairo to Luxor overnight service, which departs from Ramesses station. Where such services exist, they can be a relaxing alternative to traveling by bus or airplane and a good way of seeing some of the countryside. Interrail passes, available for 30-day train travel in participating European countries, are also valid in Morocco. Student discounts are also often available if you have an International Student Card. Be sure to check out ticket prices in advance at the station of departure. Finding out about and buying the correct tickets could take some time.

Departures

Which track [platform] to…?	أي خط إلى…؟ ay khat <u>i</u>la…
Is this the *track [platform]/ train* to…?	هل هذا الخط/القطار إلى…؟ hal <u>ha</u>za al-khat/al-qi<u>taa</u>r ila…
Where is track [platform]…?	أين خط…؟ ayn khat…
Where do I change for…?	أين أغيّر إلى…؟ ayn u<u>ha</u>yer <u>i</u>la…

Boarding

Can I *sit here/open the window*?	ممكن أجلس هنا/أفتح النافذة؟ <u>mum</u>kin <u>a</u>jlis <u>hu</u>na/<u>af</u>tah al-<u>naa</u>fiza
That's my seat.	ذلك مقعدي. <u>zaa</u>lik <u>maq</u>'adee
Here's my reservation.	ها هو حجزي. haa <u>hu</u>wa <u>Ha</u>jzee

You May Hear...

على الجميع الركوب! <u>a</u>lal jam<u>ee</u>' al-ru<u>koo</u>b	All aboard!
التذاكر، من فضلك. al-ta<u>zaa</u>kir min <u>fad</u>lak	Tickets, please.
عليك أن تغير عند... '<u>aalay</u>ik an tu<u>ghaye</u>roo 'and...	You have to change at...
المحطة القادمة... al-ma<u>Ha</u>ta al-<u>qaa</u>dima...	Next stop...

Bus

Where's the bus station?	أين محطة الباص؟ ayn ma<u>Ha</u>tat al-b<u>aas</u>
How far is it?	كم هي بعيدة؟ kam <u>hi</u>ya ba'<u>ee</u>da
How do I get to...?	كيف أصل إلى...؟ kayf <u>a</u>sil <u>i</u>la...
Is this the bus to...?	هل يذهب هذا الباص إلى...؟ hal <u>yaz</u>-hab <u>ha</u>za al-b<u>aas i</u>la...
Can you tell me when to get off?	ممكن تقول لي متى أنزل؟ <u>mum</u>kin ta<u>gool</u> lee <u>ma</u>ta <u>an</u>zil
Do I have to change buses?	هل عليّ تبديل الباص؟ hal <u>a</u>lay tab<u>deel</u> al-b<u>aas</u>
Stop here, please!	قف هنا، مِن فضلك! qif <u>hu</u>na min <u>fad</u>lak

▶ For ticketing, see page 19.

Long-distance buses are a popular means of transportation in the region and cover far more destinations than the train network. They are usually cheap and fairly reliable, but can be crowded. You may have to reserve in advance to ensure you get a seat. Make your reservations at the station if you are traveling within the same country. Go to a travel agency if you are traveling to another country.

27

You May See...

محطة باص maHatat baas	bus stop
مدخل/مخرج madkhal/makhraj	enter/exit
أختم تذكرتك ukhtum tazkaratak	stamp your ticket

i

Another popular means of long-distance travel is the سرفيس (serVees), shared taxi or microbus, which is the middle ground between long-distance buses and private taxis. These run between towns from known starting points and usually seat seven to ten people paying a fixed fare. Each *servees* will wait until it is full and then depart. If the wait is very long, it is possible for the existing passengers to agree to share the cost of the empty seats. Buses and sometimes trams are a cheap way to travel around cities, but you may want to avoid them during the crowded rush hours. You might find the bus number in English, but the destination is often written only in Arabic script, so you'll need to ask around to find the correct bus.

Subway [Underground]

Where's the subway [underground] station?	أين محطة مترو الأنفاق؟ ayn maHatat metro al-anfaaq
A map, please.	خـريطة، من فضلك. khareeta min fadlak
Which line for...?	أي خط إلى...؟ ay khat ila...
Which direction?	أي اتجاه؟ ay itijaah
Do I have to transfer [change]?	هل علي أن أغيّر؟ hal alay an ooghayer
Is this the subway [train] to...?	هل يذهب هذا القطار إلى...؟ hal yaz-hab haza al-qitaar ila...

How many stops to…?	كم محطة إلى...؟ kam maHata ila…
Where are we?	أين نحن؟ ayn naHna

▶ For ticketing, see page 19.

> *i* Cairo has a modern subway. The single line runs for over 40 kilometers from the southern suburb of Helwan, through the center and out to the northeast suburbs. Further extensions are planned. It is an efficient, clean and cheap way to travel.

Boat and Ferry

When is the ferry to…?	متى العبّارة إلى...؟ mata al-'ebaara ila…
Where are the life jackets?	أين سترات النجاة؟ ayn sitraat al-najaah

▶ For ticketing, see page 19.

You May See...

قارب النجاة qaarib al-najaah	life boat
سترة النجاة sitrat al-najaah	life jacket

> *i* There are numerous ferries operating to and among Middle Eastern countries, across the Mediterranean, the Red Sea and the Persian Gulf. Taking a ferry is usually an economical choice. A cruise down the Nile is a perennial favorite. Many boats operate between Luxor and Aswan. Check with your travel agent or the Egyptian tourist office for details about cruises currently available.

Bicycle and Motorcycle

I'd like to rent [hire]...	أريد أن أستأجـر... ‏ooreed an asta'ajir...
– a bicycle	دراجة ‏daraaja
– a moped	دراجة بمحـرك ‏daraaja bi-muHarik
– a motorcycle	دراجة نارية ‏daraaja naareeya
How much per *day/week*?	كم باليوم/الأسبوع؟ ‏kam *bil-yohm/ bil-usboo'*
Can I have a *helmet/lock*?	ممكن تعطيني خوذة/قفل؟ ‏mumkin tu'ateenee *khouza/qifl*

Bicycles can be rented in many tourist resorts and are often a fun and cheap alternative to taxis. Look for rental places in the street or ask at your hotel.

Taxi

Where can I get a taxi?	أين ممكن أن أجد تاكسي؟ ‏ayn mumkin an ajid taksee
Do you have the number for a taxi?	هل عندك رقم تاكسي؟ ‏hal 'aandak raqm taksee
I'd like a taxi...	أريد تاكسي ‏ooreed taksee
– now	الآن ‏al-'aan
– in an hour	بعد ساعة ‏ba'ad sa'aa
– for tomorrow at...	للغد الساعة... ‏lil-ghad al-sa'aa...
Pick me up at...	تعال لتأخذني الساعة... ‏ta'aala li-ta'akhuznee al-sa'aa...
I'm going to...	أنا ذاهب إلى... ‏ana zaahib ila...
– this address	هذا العنوان ‏haza al-'unwaan
– the airport	المطار ‏al-mataar
– the train [railway] station	محطة القطار ‏maHatat al-qitaar

I'm late.	أنا متأخـر <u>ana</u> muta'<u>a</u>khir
Can you drive *faster/slower*?	ممكن تسوق بسـرعة أكبر/بتمهل أكثر <u>mum</u>kin tasooq bi-<u>sur</u>'a <u>ak</u>bar/ bi-tama<u>hul</u> ak<u>tar</u>
Stop/Wait here.	قف/انتظر هنا. <u>qif/intazar</u> huna
How much?	بكم؟ bi-kam
You said it would cost…	أنت قلت أنها ستكلف… <u>an</u>ta <u>qul</u>ta <u>in</u>aha sa-tuk<u>a</u>lif…
Keep the change.	الباقي لك. al-<u>baaqee</u> lak

You May Hear...

إلى أين؟ <u>ila</u> ayn
ما هو العنوان؟ maa <u>huwa</u> al-'un<u>waan</u>
هناك أجرة إضافية للفترة الليلية/للمطار. hu<u>naak</u> ujra idaa<u>feeya</u> lil-<u>fitra</u> al-lay<u>leeya</u>/ lil-ma<u>taar</u>

Where to?
What's the address?
There's a *nighttime/ airport* surcharge.

The expected tip is 10%. Prices can be negotiated in some countries, but it is always best to agree on the price before getting into the taxi and setting off.

Car

Car Rental [Hire]

Where's the car rental [hire]?	أين إيجار السيارات؟ ayn ee<u>jaar</u> al-sayaar<u>aat</u>
I'd like…	أريد… oo<u>reed</u>…
– an automatic/a manual	بغيار عادي/بغيار أوتوماتيكي bi-ghi<u>yar</u> 'aadee/bi-ghi<u>yar</u> otom<u>a</u>teekee
– air conditioning	تكييف هواء tak<u>yeef</u> ha<u>wa'</u>
– a car seat	مقعد سيارة <u>maq</u>'ad say<u>aa</u>ra

How much...?	...بكم؟	bi-kam...
– per day/week	باليوم/بالإسبوع	bil-yohm/bil-usboo'
– per kilometer	بالكيلومتر	bil-kilometer
– for unlimited mileage	بأميال غير محدودة	bi-amyaal ghayr maHdooda
– with insurance	مع تأمين	ma' ta'ameen
Are there any discounts?	هل هناك أي تخفيضات؟	hal hunaak ay takhfeedaat

You May Hear...

هل لديكَ رخصة قيادة دولية؟ hal ladayk rukhsat qeeyaada doowaleeya	Do you have an international driver's license?
جواز سفرك من فضلك. jawaaz safrak min fadlak	Your passport, please.
هل تريد تأمين؟ hal tureed ta'ameen	Do you want insurance?
سأحتاج إلى عربون sa-aHtaaj ila 'aarboon	I'll need a deposit.
ضع الحرف الأول من اسمك/وقّع هنا da' al-Hurf al-awal min esmak/waqe' huna	*Initial/Sign* here.

Renting a car is possible in most towns, but it is often expensive. It may be possible to rent a car with an English-speaking driver, either through your hotel or a travel agent. Having your own car can be an advantage in some parts of the Middle East, for example Saudi Arabia and the Gulf states, but you might find it easier to use other available means of transportation. Women are not allowed to drive in Saudi Arabia, although exceptions are made for foreign visitors. You will need an international driver's license for all countries in the region. Minimum driving ages vary. You may want to consider hiring a local driver.

Gas [Petrol] Station

Where's the gas [petrol] station?	أين محطة البنزين؟ ayn maHatat al-benzeen
Fill it up.	إملأه. emlaahu
I'll pay *in cash/by credit card*.	سأدفع كاش/ببطاقة إئتمان. sa-adfa' *cash/bi-bitaaqat e'atimaan*

▶ For numbers, see page 168.

You May See...

بنزيـن benzeen	gas [petrol]
برصاص bi-rasaas	leaded
بدون رصاص bi-dooni rasaas	unleaded
عادي 'aadee	regular
ممتاز mumtaaz	super
الأفضل al-afdal	premium
ديزل deezil	diesel
خدمة ذاتية khedma zateeya	self-service
خدمة كاملة khedma kaamila	full-service

Asking Directions

Is this the way to...?	هل هذا الطريق إلى...؟ hal haza al-tareeq ila...
How far is it to...?	ما بعد المسافة إلى...؟ maa bu'd al-masaafa ila...

Where's...?	أين...؟ ayn...
–...Street	شارع... ...shaare'
– this address	هذا العنوان haza al-'unwaan
– the highway [motorway]	الطريق السريع al-tareeq al-saree'a
Can you show me on the map?	ممكن ترشدني على الخريطة؟ mumkin turshidnee 'alal-khareeta
I'm lost.	أنا تائه. ana taa'eh

You May Hear...

على طول ala tool	straight ahead
يسار yasaar	left
يمين yameen	right
على/حول الزاوية 'al/Hohl al-zaaweeya	on/around the corner
مقابل muqaabil	opposite
خلف khalf	behind
بجانب bi-jaanib	next to
بعد ba'ad	after
شمال/جنوب shomaal/janoob	north/south
شرق/غرب sharq/gharb	east/west
عند إشارة المرور 'and eshaarat al-muroor	at the traffic light
عند ملتقى الطرق 'and multaqee al-turuq	at the intersection

You May See...

قف qif	stop
أعط أحقية الطريق a'ett aHageeyat al-tareeq	yield [give way]
موقف mohqif	parking
ممنوع الوقوف mamnoo'a al-wuqoof	no parking
منعطف خطر mun'aatif khatar	dangerous curve
أعمال طرق aa'amaal turuk	road work
اتجاه واحد ettejaah waaHid	one way
ممنوع الدخول mamnoo'a al-dukhool	no entry
طريق مغلق tareeq mughlaq	road closed
طريق برسم مرور tareeq bi-rasm muroor	toll road
ممنوع العبور mamnoo'a al-'uboor	no passing
ممنوع الرجوع على الطريق mamnoo'a al-rujoo'a 'alal-tareeq	no U-turn
أمامك إشارات مرور amaamak eshaarat muroor	traffic signal ahead
دوار dawaar	traffic circle [roundabout]
تحويلة taHweela	detour
مخرج makhraj	exit
أدخل في السير edkhul feel-sayr	merge
إبقى في المسار ebqa feel-masaar	stay in lane
جسر منخفض jisr munkhafaz	low bridge
استخدم الضوء العالي estakhdim al-doh' al-'aalee	use headlights
عبور مشاة 'uboor mushaah	pedestrian crosswalk [crossing]

Parking

Can I park here?	ممكن أركن سيارتي هنا؟ <u>mum</u>kin <u>ar</u>kun say<u>aa</u>ratee <u>hu</u>na
Where's…?	أين…؟ ayn…
– the parking garage	موقف جراج <u>moh</u>qif ga<u>raaj</u>
– the parking lot [car park]	موقف السيارات <u>moh</u>qif al-saya<u>raat</u>
– the parking meter	عداد الموقف a<u>daad</u> al-<u>moh</u>qif
How much…?	كم…؟ kam…
– per hour	بالساعة bil-<u>saa</u>'a
– per day	باليوم bil-yohm
– overnight	بالليلة bil-<u>lay</u>la

ممنوع الوقوف
NO PARKING

Parking is usually a question of survival of the fittest and double-parking is common—although most town centers do have restrictions. Many of the larger hotels will have their own parking lots for the use of their guests.

Breakdown and Repairs

My car *broke down/ won't start.*	سيارتي تعطلت/لا تعمل. sayaaratee *ta'atalat/laa ta'amal*
Can you fix it (today)?	هل يمكن أن تصلحها(اليوم)؟ hal yumkin an tu<u>sa</u>liHha (al-yohm)
When will it be ready?	متى ستكون جاهزة؟ <u>ma</u>ta sa-<u>ta</u>kun <u>jaa</u>hiza
How much?	بكم؟ bi-kam

Accidents

There was an accident.	وقع حادث. <u>wa</u>qa' Haadis
Call *an ambulance/ the police.*	اتصل بالإسعاف/بالشرطة *it<u>a</u>sil bi al-es'aaf/al-shurta*

37

Accommodations

Essential

Can you recommend a hotel?	ممكن تنصحني بفندق؟ <u>mum</u>kin tan<u>saH</u>nee bi-<u>fun</u>duq
What is it near?	قريب من أين؟ qa<u>reeb</u> min ayn
I have a reservation.	عندي حجز. '<u>aan</u>dee Hajz
My name is...	إسمي... <u>is</u>mee...
Do you have a room...?	عندك غرفة...؟ '<u>aan</u>dak <u>ghur</u>fa...
– for one/for two	لواحد/لاثنين li-<u>waa</u>hid/li-it<u>nayn</u>
– with a bathroom	مع حمّام maa' Ha<u>maam</u>
– with air conditioning	بتكييف هواء bi-tak<u>yeef</u> ha<u>waa</u>
For...	لـ... li...
– tonight	الليلة al-<u>lay</u>la
– two nights	ليلتين layla<u>tayn</u>
– one week	أسبوع us<u>boo</u>'
How much?	بكم؟ bi-kam
Is there anything cheaper?	هل يوجد أي شيء أرخص؟ hal <u>yoo</u>jad ay shay <u>ar</u>khas
Can I see the room?	ممكن أرى الغرفة؟ <u>mum</u>kin <u>a</u>ra al-<u>ghur</u>fa
I'll take it.	سآخذها. sa-aa<u>khud</u>-haa
When's check-out?	متى وقت تسليم الغرفة؟ <u>ma</u>ta waqt tas<u>leem</u> al-<u>ghur</u>fa
Can I leave this in the safe?	ممكن أترك هذا في الخزينة؟ <u>mum</u>kin <u>a</u>truk <u>haa</u>za feel-kha<u>zee</u>na
Can I leave my bags?	ممكن أترك حقائبي؟ <u>mum</u>kin <u>a</u>truk Ha<u>qaa</u>'ibee

Can I have *my bill/a receipt*?   <u>mum</u>kin al-*Hisaab*/*eesaal* ممكن الحساب/إيصال؟

I'll pay *in cash/ by credit card*.   sa-<u>ad</u>faa *cash*/*bitaaqat e'atimaan* سأدفع كاش/ببطاقة إئتمان.

Is there a campsite nearby?   hal hu<u>naak</u> mu<u>khay</u>yam qa<u>reeb</u> هل هناك مخيّم قريب؟

i

If you didn't reserve accommodations before your trip, visit the local Tourist Information Office مكتب الاستعلامات السياحية (<u>mak</u>tab al-este'ala<u>maat</u> al-seeyaa<u>Hee</u>ya) for recommendations on places to stay. Many Arabic countries/cities have their own websites in English.

Finding Lodgings

Can you recommend...?	ممكن تنصحني...؟ <u>mum</u>kin tan<u>saH</u>nee...
– a hotel	بفندق bi-<u>fun</u>duq
– a hostel/youth hostel	بـنـزُل/بيت شباب bi-<u>nuz</u>ul/ bayt she<u>baab</u>
– a campsite	بمخيّم bi-mu<u>khay</u>yam
What is it near?	قريب من أين؟ qa<u>reeb</u> min ayn
How do I get there?	كيف أصل هناك؟ kayf <u>asil</u> hun<u>aak</u>

i There is a wide range of accommodations to choose from in the Middle East, from luxury Western-style hotels to youth hostels, rented apartments and camp sites. Try to reserve in advance, particularly during local holidays. In many parts of the Middle East, an unmarried man and woman will not be allowed to share a room, although two men or two women should pose no problem. Women traveling alone should be especially careful to reserve accommodations in an international or otherwise well-known hotel. Accommodations in hostels or campsites are most likely to be found in countries such as Algeria, Morocco and Egypt.

At the Hotel

I have a reservation.	عندي حجز. '<u>aan</u>dee Hajz
My name is...	إسمي... <u>is</u>mee...
Do you have a room...?	عندك غـرفة؟ '<u>aan</u>dak <u>ghur</u>fa
– with a *bathroom [toilet]/ shower*	مع حمّام/دُش maa' *Hamaam/doosh*
– with air conditioning	بتكييف هواء bi-tak<u>yeef</u> ha<u>waa</u>
– that's *smoking/ non-smoking*	للمدخنين/لغير المدخنين lil-*modakh-* <u>eneen</u>/ghayr al-modakh<u>eneen</u>

For...	...لـ li...
– tonight	الليلة lil-<u>lay</u>la
– two nights	ليلتين layla<u>tayn</u>
– a week	أسبوع us<u>boo</u>'

▶ For numbers, see page 168.

Do you have...?	هل عـندَك...؟ hal <u>aan</u>dak...
– a computer	كمبيوتر kamp<u>yoo</u>ter
– an elevator [a lift]	مصعـد <u>mis</u>'ad
– (wireless) internet service	خدمة إنترنت (لاسلكي) <u>khed</u>mat internet (laasil<u>kee</u>)
– housekeeping services	خدمات تنظيف khed<u>maat</u> tan<u>zeef</u>
– laundry service	خدمة غسيل ملابس <u>khed</u>mat gha<u>seel</u> ma<u>laa</u>bis
– room service	خدمة غـرف <u>khed</u>mat <u>ghu</u>ruf
– a TV	تلفزيون televizi<u>yoon</u>
– a pool	مسبح <u>mas</u>baH
– a gym	جيمنازيوم jimn<u>aa</u>ziyoom
I need an extra bed/ a crib [cot].	أحتاج إلى سرير إضافي/سرير للرضيع. aH<u>taaj</u> ila <u>sareer</u> e<u>daa</u>fee/<u>sareer</u> al-ra<u>dee</u>'a

You May Hear...

جواز سفرك/بطاقة إئتمانك، من فضلك. ja<u>waaz</u> <u>saf</u>rak/bi<u>taa</u>qat e'ati<u>maa</u>nak min <u>fad</u>lak	Your *passport/ credit card*, please.
إملأ هذه الإستمارة، <u>im</u>la <u>ha</u>za al-esti<u>maa</u>ra	Fill out this form.
وقّع هنا. <u>wa</u>qeh <u>hu</u>na	Sign here.

Price

How much per *night/week*?	كم في الليلة/الأسبوع؟ kam fee *al-layla/al-usboo'*
Does that include…?	هل يشمل هذا…؟ hal yashmal haza…
– breakfast	الفطور al-futoor
– housekeeping service	خدمة التنظيف khedmat al-tanzeef
– sales tax [VAT]	الضريبة al-dareeba
Do I have to leave a deposit?	هل أحتاج لدفع عـربون؟ hal aHtaaj li-dafa' aaraboon
Are there any discounts?	هل هناك تخفيضات؟ hal hunaak takhfeedaat

Decisions

Can I see the room?	ممكن أرى الغرفة؟ mumkin ara al-ghurfa
I'd like…room.	أريد غـرفة… ooreed ghurfa…
– a better	أفضل afdal
– a bigger	أكبر akbar
– a cheaper	أرخـص arkhas
– a quieter	أهدأ ahda
I'll take it.	سآخذها sa-aakhud-haa
No, I won't take it.	لا, لن آخذها. laa lan aakhud-haa

Questions

Where's…?	أين…؟ ayn…
– the bar	البار al-baar
– the bathroom [toilet]	التواليت al-toowaaleet

– the dining room	غرفة الطعام <u>ghur</u>fat al-ta'<u>aam</u>
– the elevator [lift]	المصعد al-<u>mis</u>'ad
– the kitchen	المطبخ al-<u>mat</u>bakh
– the parking lot [car park]	جراج السيارات ga<u>raaj</u> as-saya<u>raat</u>
– the pool	المسبح al-<u>mas</u>baH
Can I have…?	ممكن آخذ…؟ <u>mum</u>kin <u>aa</u>khud…
– a blanket	بطانية bata<u>nee</u>ya
– an iron	مكواة <u>mik</u>wa
– the *room key/key card*	كرت المفتاح/مفتاح الغرفة *kart al miftaH/miftaH al-ghur*fa
– a pillow	مخدة mi<u>khad</u>da
– soap	صابون saa<u>boon</u>
– toilet paper	ورق تواليت <u>wa</u>raq toowaa<u>leet</u>
– a towel	منشفة <u>min</u>shafa
Do you have an adapter for this?	هل عندك محوّل لهذا؟ hal <u>aan</u>dak mu<u>Haw</u>wil li-<u>ha</u>za
How do I turn on the lights?	كيف أشعل النور؟ kayf <u>ash</u>'al al-noor
Can you wake me at…?	ممكن تصحيني الساعة…؟ <u>mum</u>kin tusa<u>Hee</u>nee al-<u>sa</u>'aa…
Can I leave this in the safe?	ممكن أترك هذا في الخزينة؟ <u>mum</u>kin <u>a</u>truk <u>ha</u>za feel kha<u>zee</u>na
Can I have my things from the safe?	ممكن آخذ أشيائي من الخزينة؟ <u>mum</u>kin <u>a</u>khud ash<u>yaa</u>'ee min al-kha<u>zee</u>na
Is there *mail [post]/ a message* for me?	هل هناك بريد/رسائل لي؟ hal hu<u>naak</u> *ba<u>reed</u>/ ra<u>saa</u>*'il lee

إسحب/إدفع esHab/edfa'	push/pull
حمّام Hamaam	bathroom [toilet]
دُش doosh	shower
مصعد mis'ad	elevator [lift]
دَرَج daraj	stairs
مكائن بيع/ثلج makaa'in bee'/talaj	ice/vending machines
غسيل ملابس ghaseel malaabis	laundry
الرجاء عـدم الإزعاج al-rijaa adam al-ez'aaj	do not disturb
مخرج الحريق makhraj al-Hareeq	fire door
مخرج (الطوارئ) makhraj (al-tawaari')	(emergency) exit
مكالمة إيقاظ mukaalamat eeqaaz	wake-up call

Problems

There's a problem.	هناك مشكلة. hunaak mushkila
I lost my *key/key card*.	فقدت مفتاحي/كرت مفتاحي. faqadtu miftaaHee/kart miftaaHee
I'm locked out of the room.	لا أستطيع الدخول إلى غـرفتي. laa astatee'a al-dukhool li-ghurfatee
There's no *hot water/toilet paper*.	لا يوجد ماء ساخن/ورق تواليت. laa yoojad maa' saakhin/waraq toowaaleet
The room is dirty.	الغرفة وسخة. al-ghurfa wisikha
There are bugs in the room.	هناك حشرات في الغرفة. hunaak Hasharaat feel-ghurfa
The...doesn't work.	لا يعمل... laa...ya'amal

Can you fix...?	يمكنك تصليح...؟ yumkinak tasleeH...
– the air conditioning	تكييف الهواء takyeef al-hawaa
– the fan	المروحة al-marwaHa
– the heat [heating]	التدفئة al-tadfi'a
– the light	الضوء al-dhow
– the TV	التلفزيون al-televiziyoon
– the toilet	التواليت al-toowaaleet
I'd like another room.	أريد غرفة أخرى. ooreed ghurfa ookhra

In most Middle Eastern countries, the electric current is 220 volts AC, but there are variations. There are many different types of sockets and plugs in use, so it is best to take a universal adapter with you. In some countries, you could experience power cuts and may want to take a flashlight for emergencies.

Check-out

When's check-out?	متى وقت تسليم الغرفة؟ mata waqt tasleem al-ghurfa
Can I leave my bags here until...?	ممكن أترك حقائبي هنا حتى...؟ mumkin atruk Haqaa'ibee huna Hata...
Can I have *an itemized bill/a receipt*?	ممكن تعطيني قائمة مفصلة بالحساب/الوصل؟ mumkin ta'ateenee *qaa'ima mufassala bil-Hisaab/ al-wasl*
I think there's a mistake	أعتقد أن هناك خطأ. a'aataqed an hunaak khata'
I'll pay *in cash/ by credit card.*	سأدفع كاش/ببطاقة إئتمان. sa-adfaa *cash/bitaaqat e'atimaan*

45

Renting

I reserved *an apartment/ a room.*	أنا حجزت شقة/غرفة. <u>an</u>a Ha<u>jaz</u>atu *shiqqa/ ghurfa*
My name is…	إسمي… <u>is</u>mee…
Can I have the *key/ key card*?	ممكن آخذ المفتاح/كرت المفتاح؟ <u>mum</u>kin <u>aa</u>khuz *al-miftaaH/kart al-miftaaH*
Are there…?	هل هناك…؟ hal hu<u>naak</u>…
– dishes	صحون su<u>Hoon</u>
– pillows	مخدات mikha<u>daat</u>
– sheets	ملايات mila<u>yaat</u>
– towels	مناشف ma<u>naa</u>shif
– utensils	أدوات الطبخ ada<u>waat</u> al-tabkh
When do I put out the trash [rubbish]?	متى أخرج الزبالة؟ <u>mata</u> <u>ukh</u>rij al-zi<u>baa</u>la
How does the…work?	كيف يعمل الـ…؟ kayf <u>ya</u>'amal al-…
The…is broken.	الـ…مكسور al-…maksoor
– air conditioner	تكييف الهواء tak<u>yeef</u> al-ha<u>waa</u>
– dishwasher	غسالة الصحون gha<u>saa</u>lat al-su<u>Hoon</u>
– freezer	فريزر fi<u>ree</u>zir
– heater [heating]	سخان sa<u>khaan</u>
– microwave	ميكرويف <u>mee</u>kroowayif

| – refrigerator | ثلاجة tal<u>laaj</u>a |
| – stove | فرن furn |

▶ For oven temperatures, see page 176.

| – washing machine | غسالة الملابس gha<u>saal</u>at al-ma<u>laab</u> |

Household Items

I need...	أحتاج... aH<u>taaj</u>...
– an adapter	محوّل mu<u>Haww</u>il
– aluminum [kitchen] foil	رقائق المنيوم ra<u>qaa</u>'iq alu<u>min</u>yoom
– a bottle opener	فتاحة زجاجات fa<u>taa</u>Hat zujaa<u>jaat</u>
– a broom	مكنسة <u>mik</u>nasa
– a can opener	فتاحة معلبات fa<u>taa</u>Hat mu'ala<u>baat</u>
– cleaning supplies	مواد تنظيف ma<u>waad</u> tan<u>zeef</u>
– a corkscrew	فتاحة النبيذ fa<u>taa</u>Hat al-na<u>beet</u>
– detergent	منظف mu<u>nazz</u>if
– dishwashing liquid	سائل لغسيل الصحون <u>saa</u>'il li-gha<u>seel</u> al-su<u>Hoon</u>
– garbage [rubbish] bags	أكياس قمامة ak<u>yaas</u> qa<u>maam</u>a
– a lightbulb	لمبة <u>lamb</u>a
– matches	كبريت kib<u>reet</u>
– a mop	ممسحة <u>mim</u>saHa
– napkins	مناديل المائدة mana<u>deel</u> al-<u>maa</u>'ida
– paper towels	مناشف ورق ma<u>naash</u>if <u>waraq</u>
– plastic wrap [cling film]	غلاف نايلون ghi<u>laaf</u> nay<u>loon</u>
– a plunger	الغاطس al-<u>ghaat</u>is
– scissors	مقـ ص mi<u>qass</u>

▶ For dishes and utensils, see page 68.

Hostel

Is there a bed available?	هل يوجد سرير فارغ؟ hal <u>yoo</u>jad sa<u>reer</u> <u>faa</u>regh
Can I have…?	ممكن آخذ…؟ <u>mum</u>kin <u>aa</u>khud…
– a *single/double* room	غرفة منفردة/مزدوّجة <u>ghur</u>fa mun<u>fa</u>reda/ muz<u>dow</u>aja
– a blanket	بطانية bataa<u>nee</u>ya
– a pillow	مخدة mi<u>kha</u>dda
– sheets	ملايات milaa<u>ya</u>at
– a towel	منشفة <u>min</u>shafa
Do you have lockers?	هل عندك خزائن؟ hal <u>aan</u>dak kha<u>zaa</u>'in
When do you lock up?	متى تقفل؟ <u>ma</u>ta <u>taq</u>ful
Do I need a membership card?	هل أحتاج إلى كرت عضوية؟ hal a<u>H</u>taaj <u>il</u>a kart uz<u>wee</u>ya
Here's my International Student Card.	ها هو كرتي الطلابي العالمي <u>ha</u> <u>hu</u>wa <u>kar</u>tee al-tu<u>laa</u>bee al-'aalemee

Youth hostels بيت شباب (bayt sha<u>baab</u>) can be found in some Arab countries, including Morocco, Egypt, Bahrain, Qatar and Saudi Arabia. You may need a Hostelling International card to get a discount.

Camping

Can I camp here?	ممكن أخيّم هنا؟ <u>mum</u>kin oo<u>kha</u>yem <u>hu</u>na
Where's the campsite?	أين المخيّم؟ ayn al-mo<u>kha</u>yam
What is the charge per *day/week*?	كم باليوم/بالأسبوع؟ kam bil-yohm/ bil-us<u>boo</u>'

Are there...?	هل هناك...؟ hal hunaak...
– cooking facilities	لوازم طبخ lawaazim tabkh
– electric outlets	مآخذ كهرباء ma'akhaz kahrabaa'
– laundry facilities	مغسلة maghsala
– showers	دُش doosh
– tents for rent [hire]	خيام للإيجار khayaam lil-eejaar
Can I have...?	ممكن آخذ...؟ mumkin aakhud...
– some cooking gas	قليلاً من غاز الطبخ qaleelan min gaz al-tabkh
– some charcoal	قليلاً من الفحم qaleelan min al-faHam
– a flashlight	كشاف kashaaf
– a groundcloth [groundsheet]	حصيرة haseera
– a hammer	مطرقة mitraqa
– a camping stove	فرن مخيم furn mokhayam
– matches	كبريت kibreet
– a sleeping bag	حقيبة للنوم Haqeeba lil-nowm
– tent pegs	أوتاد لخيمة awtaad lil-khayma
– a tent pole	عامود لخيمة 'aamood lil-khayma
Where can I empty the chemical toilet?	أين يمكنني إفراغ التواليت الكميائي؟ ayn yumkinenee efraagh al-toowaaleet al-kimiyaa'ee

▶ For household items, see page 47.

▶ For dishes and utensils, see page 68.

ماء للشرب maa' lil-shurb	drinking water
ممنوع التخييم mamnoo' al-takhyeem	no camping
ممنوع إشعال النار/الشوي mamnoo' esh'aal al-naar/al-shawa	no *fires/barbecues*

i Campsites are found in some countries in the Arab world and are often in attractive locations and close to the sea. Camping outside official sites is not recommended and can lead to fines and even arrest.

Internet and Communications

Essential

Where's an internet cafe?	أين يوجد مقهى إنترنت؟ ayn yoojad maqhan internet
Can I access the internet?	ممكن أدخل على الإنترنت؟ mumkin adkhul 'alal-internet
Can I check e-mail?	ممكن أشوف البريد الإلكتروني؟ mumkin ashoof al-bareed al-elektroonee
How much per (half) hour?	كم الحساب لمدة (نصف) ساعة؟ kam al-Hisaab li-muddat (nusf) saa'aa
How do I *connect/ log on*?	كيف أصل/أدخل على الإنترنت؟ kayf asil/adkhul 'alal-internet
A phone card, please.	بطاقة تلفونية، من فضلك. bitaaqa tilifooneeya min fadlak

Can I have your phone number?	ممكن آخذ رقم تلفونك؟ <u>mum</u>kin akhz raqm tili<u>foo</u>nak
Here's my *number/e-mail*.	هذا رقمي/عنوان بريدي الإلكتروني. <u>ha</u>za <u>raq</u>mee/'un<u>waan</u> ba<u>ree</u>dee al-elek<u>troo</u>nee
Call me.	اتصل بي. it<u>ta</u>sil bee
E-mail me.	أرسل لي رسالة إلكترونية. <u>ur</u>sil lee ri<u>saa</u>la elektroo<u>nee</u>ya
Hello. This is…	السلام عليكم. أنا… al-sa<u>laam</u> 'aa<u>lay</u>kum <u>a</u>na…
Can I speak to…?	ممكن أتكلم مع…؟ <u>mum</u>kin ata<u>kal</u>lam ma'…
Can you repeat that?	ممكن تعيد؟ <u>mum</u>kin tu'<u>eed</u>
I'll call back later.	سأتصل لاحقاً. sa-at<u>ta</u>sil <u>laa</u>Hiqan
Bye.	مع السلامة. ma' al-sa<u>laa</u>ma
Where's the post office?	أين البريد؟ ayn al-ba<u>reed</u>
I'd like to send this to…	أريد أن أرسل هذا إلى… oo<u>reed</u> an <u>ur</u>sil <u>ha</u>za i<u>la</u>…

51

Computer, Internet and E-mail

Where's an internet cafe? | أين يوجد مقهى إنترنت؟ ayn yoojad maqhan internet

Does it have wireless internet? | عندهم إنترنت لاسلكي؟ 'aandahum internet laasilkee

How do I turn the computer on/off? | كيف أشغّل/أطفئ الكومبيوتر؟ kayf ushaghil/atfee al-kompyootir

Can I...? | ممكن...؟ mumkin...

– access the internet | أدخل على الإنترنت adkhul 'alal-internet

– burn CDs/DVDs | أنسخ سي دي/دي في دي ansakh CD/DVD

– check e-mail | أشوف البريد الإلكتروني ashoof al-bareed al-elektroonee

– print | أطبع atba'

– use any computer | أستخدم أي كومبيوتر astakhdim ay kompyootir

How much per (half) hour? | كم الحساب لمدة (نصف) ساعة؟ kam al-Hisaab li-muddat (nusf) saa'aa

How do I...? | كيف...؟ kayf...

– connect/disconnect | أتصل/أقطع الاتصال؟ attasil/aqta' al-ettisaal

– log on/off | أدخل على/أخرج من الإنترنت adkhul 'ala/akhruj min al-internet

– type this symbol | أطبع هذا الرمز atba' haza al-ramz

What's your e-mail? | ما هو عنوان بريدك الإلكتروني؟ maa huwa 'unwaan bareedak al-elektroonee

My e-mail is... | عنوان بريدي الإلكتروني هو... 'unwaan bareedee al-elektroonee huwa...

Do you have a scanner? | عندكم ماسحة؟ 'aandakum maasiHa

52

You May See...

إغلاق eghlaaq	close
تراجع taraaju'a	delete
بريد إلكتروني bareed elektroonee	e-mail
خروج khurooj	exit
مساعدة musaa'ada	help
ماسنجر messenger	instant messenger
إنترنت internet	internet
دخول dukhool	login
رسالة جديدة risaala jadeeda	new message
تشغيل/إيقاف tashgheel/eeqaaf	on/off
فتح fatH	open
طباعة tabaa'aa	print

حفظ Hafz	save
إرسال ersaal	send
اسم المستخدم/كلمة المرور ism al-mustakhdim/kalimat al-muroor	username/password
إنترنت لاسلكي internet laasilkee	wireless internet

Phone

A *phone card/ prepaid phone card* please.

بطاقة تلفونية/بطاقة تلفونية مسبقة الدفع، من فضلك.
bitaaqa tilifooneeya/bitaaqa tilifooneeya musabbaqat al-daf' min fadlak

An international phone card for...

بطاقة تلفونية دوليةلـ... *bitaaqa tilifooneeya duwaleeya li...*

– Australia

أستراليا ustraaleeya

– Canada

كندا kanada

– Ireland

أيرلندا irlanda

– the U.K.

بريطانيا breetaaneeya

– the U.S.

أمريكا amreeka

Can I *recharge/buy minutes for* this phone?

ممكن أشحن/أشتري وحدات لهذا التلفون؟ *mumkin ashHan/ashtaree waHdaat li-haza al-tilifoon*

My phone doesn't work here.

تلفوني لا يعمل هنا. tilifoonee laa ya'amal huna

What's the *area/country* code for...?

ما رمز المنطقة/البلد لـ...؟ maa ramz al-mantaqa/al-balad li...

What's the number for Information?

ما رقم الاستعلامات؟ maa raqm al-este'alamaat

I'd like the number for...

أريد رقم لـ.... ooreed raqm li-...

I'd like to call collect [reverse the charges].	أريد أن تكون كلفة المكالمة على المستقبل. ooreed an takoon kulfat al-mukaalama 'alal-mustaqbil
Can I have your number?	ممكن آخذ رقمك؟ mumkin akhz raqmak
Here's my number.	هذا رقمي. haza raqmee

▶ For numbers, see page 168.

Please *call/text* me.	اتصل بي/ابعث لي إس إم إس. ittasil bee/ab'as lee SMS
I'll *call/text* you.	سأتصل بك/سأبعث لك إس إم إس. sa-attasil beek/sa-ab'as lak SMS

On the Phone

Hello. This is...	السلام عليكم. أنا... al-salaam 'aalaykum ana...
Can I speak to...?	ممكن أتكلم مع...؟ mumkin atakallam ma'...
Extension...	الرقم الفرعي... al-raqm al-far'ee...
Speak *louder/more slowly*, please.	ممكن تقوي صوتك/تتكلم ببطء، من فضلك. mumkin tugawwee sohtak/tatakallam bi-but' min fadlak
Can you repeat that?	ممكن تعيد؟ mumkin tu'eed
I'll call back later.	سأتصل لاحقاً. sa-attasil laaHiqan
Bye.	مع السلامة. ma' al-salaama

You May Hear...

من المتكلم؟ man al-mutakallim	Who's calling?
لحظة من فضلك laHza min fadlak	Hold on.
سأحولك. sa-uHawwilak	I'll put you through.

هو♂/هي♀ غير موجود/على خط آخر. huwa♂/hiya♀ ghayr mohjood/'ala khat aakhar	He/She is *not here/* *on another line.*
هل تحب أن تترك له خبر؟ hal tuHib an tatruk lahu khabr	Would you like to leave a message?
اتصل لاحقاً/بعد عشر دقائق. ittasil/ aaHiqan/ba'ad 'ashr daqaa'iq	Call back *later/* *in 10 minutes.*
ممكن يرد♂/ترد♀ اتصالك لاحقاً؟ yarud♂/tarud♀ ittisaalak laaHiqan	Can he/she call you back?
ما رقم تلفونك؟ maa raqm tilifoonak	What's your number?

---

i The major cities of the Arab World are rapidly integrating into the international telephone network. Outside major cities, however, you may still have to go to a post office or telephone bureau to make international calls. Find out the rates per minute in advance. Phone cards for use in public phones are still not very common, although some Gulf states have introduced them on a limited basis. You may be able to place a long-distance call using an international phone card. E-mail and internet access in the Middle East is somewhat sporadic and ISPs may be limited to one or two state-approved companies. But internet cafes are increasingly popular in most main cities these days.

Fax

Can I *send/receive* a fax here?	ممكن أرسل/أستقبل فاكس هنا؟ mumkin ursil/astaqbil faks huna
What's the fax number?	ما رقم الفاكس؟ maa raqm al-faks
Please fax this to…	ممكن ترسل هذا بالفاكس إلى… mumkin tursil haza bil-faks ila…
How much?	كم الحساب؟ kam al-Hisaab

Post Office

Where's the *post office/mailbox* [*postbox*]?	أين البريد/صندوق البريد؟ ayn al-ba<u>reed</u>/<u>sundooq</u> al-ba<u>reed</u>
A stamp for this *postcard/letter* to…	أريد طابع لهذا الكرت/هذه الرسالة إلى… oo<u>reed</u> <u>taabe'</u> li-<u>haza</u> al-kart/<u>hazih</u> al-ri<u>saa</u>la ila…
How much?	كم الحساب kam-al-Hi<u>saab</u>
Send this package *by airmail/express.*	أرسل هذا الطرد بالبريد الجوي/بالبريد السريع <u>ur</u>sil <u>haza</u> al-tard bil-ba<u>reed</u> al-<u>joh</u>wee/ bil-ba<u>reed</u> al-sa<u>ree'</u>
When will it arrive?	متى سيصل؟ <u>mata</u> sa-<u>ya</u>sil
A receipt, please.	إيصال، من فضلك. ee<u>saal</u> min <u>fadl</u>ak

You May Hear…

.املأ التصريح الجمركي <u>emlaa'</u> al-tasreeH al-<u>jum</u>rukee	Fill out the customs declaration form.
ما قيمته؟ maa qee<u>mat</u>-hu	What's the value?
ماذا فيه؟ <u>maaza</u> <u>fee</u>hee	What's inside?

▼ Food

Eating Out

Essential

Can you recommend a good *restaurant/ bar*?	hal هل تنصحني بمطعم/ببار جيد؟ tansaHnee bi-*mat'aam*/bi-*bar* jayid
Is there a *traditional/ inexpensive* restaurant nearby?	هل هناك مطعم تقليدي/غير مكلف بالقرب من هنا؟ hal hunaak mat'aam taqleedee/ghayr muklif bil-qurb min huna
A table for…, please.	طاولة لـ…من فضلك. taawila li-…min fadlak
Can we sit…?	ممكن نجلس…؟ mumkin najlis…
– here/there	هنا/هناك huna/hunaak
– outside	في الخارج feel khaarij
– in a non-smoking area	حيث التدخين ممنوع Hays al-tadkheen mamnoo'
I'm waiting for someone.	أنا أنتظر أحداً. ana antazer aHadan
Where's the restroom [toilet]?	أين التواليت؟ ayn al-toowaleet
A menu, please.	قائمة الطعام من فضلك gaa'imat al-ta'aam min fadlak
What do you recommend?	بم تنصحني؟ bi-maa tansaHnee
I'd like…	أريد… ooreed…
Some more…, please.	المزيد من…من فضلك. al-mazeed min…min fadlak
Enjoy your meal!	صحة! saHHa
The check [bill], please.	الحساب من فضلك. al-Hisaab min fadlak

Is service included?	هل أجرة الخدمة محسوبة؟ hal ujrat al-khidma maHsooba
Can I *pay by credit card/have a receipt*?	ممكن استخدم بطاقة الائتمان/تعطيني إيصال؟ mumkin astakhdim bitaaqat al-e'atimaan/tu'teenee eesaal
Thank you!	شكراً! shukran

i Hospitality is taken very seriously in the Middle East. If you are invited out to a meal in a restaurant you would not be expected to pay, nor should you try! If you are invited to a meal in someone's home you should take a gift—a cake, chocolates or something for the house. Expect to have your plate piled high and to be bombarded with constant encouragements to have more. A polite way of refusing is to say دايمة (daymeh) or "always," which roughly means "may you always be in a position to provide such a sumptuous meal".

Restaurant Types

Can you recommend...?	ممكن تنصحني بـ...؟ mumkin tansaHnee bi-...
– a restaurant	مطعم mat'am
– a bar	بار baar
– a bean and falafel stand	محل فول و فلافل maHall fool wa falaafil
– a cafe	مقهى maqha
– a dessert shop	حلواني Halawaanee
– a fast-food place	مطعم للوجبات السريعة mat'am lil-wajabaat al-saree'a
– a Lebanese restaurant	كأس عرق و مزة kaa's 'aaraq wa mazza
– a snack bar	مطعم للوجبات الخفيفة mat'am lil-wajabaat al-khafeefa

Restaurants range from the very expensive to the budget end of the market, often offering a mixture of western and Middle Eastern dishes. Meals are later than in North America or Northern Europe. However, whenever you get hungry you can try bean and falafel stands, dessert shops or cafes; these are generally open day and night.

Breakfast الفطور (al-fu<u>t</u>oor) is served between 6 and 10 a.m. in most hotels. Lunch الغذاء (al-gha<u>daa</u>') is the main meal of the day, usually eaten between 1 and 3:30 p.m. Dinner العشاء (al-'aashaa) is usually eaten between 8 and 11 p.m. (or even later) and can be a lighter version of lunch or a snack, such as fa<u>teer</u> (pancake).

Reservations and Questions

I'd like to reserve a table...	أريد أن أحجز طاولة... ooreed an aHjuz taawala...
– for 2	لشخصين li-shakhsayn
– for this evening	لهذا المساء li-haza al-masaa'
– for tomorrow at...	ليوم غد الساعة... li-yohm ghadin al-saa'ah...
A table for 2, please.	طاولة لشخصين من فضلك. taawala li-shakhsayn min fadlak
We have a reservation.	عندنا حجز. 'aandana Hajz
My name is...	اسمي... esmee...
Can we sit...?	ممكن نجلس...؟ mumkin najlis...
– here/there	هنا/هناك huna/hunaak
– outside	في الخارج feel khaarij
– in a non-smoking area	حيث التدخين ممنوع Hays al-tadkheen mamnoo'
– by the window	بالقرب من النافذة. bil-qurb min al-naafiza
Where's the restroom [toilet]?	أين التواليت؟ ayn al-toowaleet

You May Hear...

عندك حجز؟ 'aandak Hajz	Do you have a reservation?
كم شخص؟ kam shakhs	How many?
هل تدخن؟ hal tudakhin	Smoking or non-smoking?
جاهز للطلب؟ jaahiz lil-talb	Are you ready to order?
ماذا تحب؟ maaza tuHib	What would you like?
أنصحك بـ... ansaHak bi...	I recommend...
صحة! saHHa	Enjoy your meal.

Ordering

Waiter/Waitress!	يا غرسون/يا آنسة! ya gharsoon/ ya aanisa
We're ready to order.	نحن جاهزون للطلب. naHna jaahizoon lil-talb
The wine list, please.	قائمة النبيذ من فضلك. qaa'imat al-nabeez min fadlak
I'd like...	أريد... ooreed...
– a bottle of...	زجاجة... zajaajat...
– a carafe of...	إبريق... ebreeq...
– a glass of...	كأس... ka's...

▶ For alcoholic and non-alcoholic drinks, see page 79.

The menu, please.	قائمة الطعام من فضلك. qaa'imat al-ta'aam min fadlak
Do you have...?	عندكم...؟ 'aandakum...
– a menu in English	قائمة طعام بالإنكليزي qaa'imat ta'aam bil-engleezee
– a fixed-price menu	قائمة طعام مع الأسعار qaa'imat ta'aam ma' al-as'aar
– a children's menu	قائمة طعام للأطفال qaa'imat ta'aam lil-atfaal
What do you recommend?	بم تنصحني؟ bi-maa tansaHnee
What's this?	ما هذا؟ maa haza
What's in it?	مم يتكون هذا؟ mimaa yatakawan haza
Is it spicy?	هل هو حار؟ hal huwa Haar
Without..., please.	بدون...من فضلك. bi-doon...min fadlak
It's to go [take away].	سآخذ الوجبة معي. sa-aakhuz al-wajba ma'ee

You May See...

رسم الخدمة rasm al-<u>kh</u>idma	cover charge
سعر محدد si'r mu<u>H</u>adad	fixed-price
قائمة الطعام <u>q</u>aa'imat al-ta'<u>aa</u>m	menu
طبق اليوم <u>t</u>abaq al-yohm	menu of the day
أجرة الخدمة غير محسوبة ujrat al-<u>kh</u>idma <u>gh</u>ayr ma<u>H</u>s<u>oo</u>ba	service (not) included
أطباق إضافية a<u>t</u>b<u>aa</u>q edaaf<u>ee</u>ya	side dishes
أطباق خاصة a<u>t</u>b<u>aa</u>q <u>kh</u>aasa	specials

Cooking Methods

baked	في الفرن feel furn
boiled	مسلوق masl<u>oo</u>q
braised	مدمس mu<u>d</u>am</u>mas
breaded	مكسي بالخبز <u>mak</u>see bil-<u>kh</u>ubz
creamed	مهروس <u>mah</u>roos
diced	مكعبات muka'<u>a</u>baat
fileted	فيليه feel<u>ay</u>
fried	مقلي <u>maq</u>lee
grilled	مشوي <u>mash</u>wee
poached	بوشيه boo<u>shay</u>
roasted	محمص mu<u>Ham</u>mas
sautéed	سوتيه soh<u>tay</u>
smoked	مدخن mu<u>da</u>khan
steamed	على البخار 'alal-bu<u>khaar</u>
stewed	مطهو بالغلي البطيء mat-<u>hoo</u> bil-<u>gh</u>alee al-ba<u>t</u>ee'
stuffed	محشي mu<u>H</u>shee

Special Requirements

I'm… أنا... <u>a</u>na…

– diabetic مريض♂/مريضة♀ بالسكري mareed♂/ mareeda♀ bil-su<u>ka</u>ree

– lactose intolerant أتحسس من اللاكتوز ataHasas min al-lak<u>too</u>z

– vegetarian نباتي♂/نباتية♀ na<u>baa</u>tee♂/nabateeya♀

I'm allergic to… أتحسس من.... ataHasas min…

I can't eat… لا أستطيع أن آكل... laa asta<u>tee</u>' an <u>a</u>kul…

– dairy منتجات الألبان munta<u>jaat</u> al-al<u>baan</u>

– gluten الغلوتين al ghl<u>oo</u>teen

– nuts المكسرات al-mukass<u>araat</u>

– pork لحم الخنزير laHm al-khan<u>zeer</u>

– shellfish المأكولات البحرية الصدفية al-ma'akoo<u>laat</u> al-baH<u>ree</u>ya al-sada<u>fee</u>ya

– spicy foods الأطعمة الحارة al-<u>at</u>'ima al-<u>Haa</u>ra

– wheat القمح al-<u>qa</u>maH

Is it halal? هل هو حلال؟ hal <u>huwa</u> Ha<u>laal</u>

Dining with Kids

Do you have children's portions? عندكم وجبات أصغر للأطفال؟ '<u>aan</u>dakum waja<u>baat</u> asghar lil-atfaal

A *highchair/child's seat*, please. كرسي خاص للأطفال/كرسي عال فضلك. <u>kur</u>see <u>k</u>haas lil-at<u>faal/kur</u>see '<u>aa</u>lin min fad<u>lak</u>

Where can I *feed/change* the baby? أين أستطيع إطعام/تغيير حفاض الطفل؟ ayn asta<u>tee</u>' et'<u>aam/tau</u>hyee<u>r</u> Hi<u>faad</u> al-tifl

| Can you warm this? | ممكن تسخن هذا؟ <u>mum</u>kin tu<u>sa</u>khin <u>ha</u>za |

▶ For travel with children, see page 144.

Complaints

How much longer will our food be?	كم ستتأخر وجبتنا؟ kam sa-tata'<u>a</u>khar waj<u>ba</u>tna
We can't wait any longer.	لا نستطيع الانتظار أكثر. laa nasta<u>tee</u>' al-enti<u>zaar</u> <u>ak</u>tar
We're leaving.	نحن ذاهبون. na<u>H</u>na zahi<u>boon</u>
I didn't order this.	أنا لم أطلب هذا. <u>a</u>na lam <u>at</u>lub <u>ha</u>za
I ordered…	أنا طلبت… <u>a</u>na ta<u>lab</u>tu…
I can't eat this.	لا أستطيع أن آكل هذا. laa asta<u>tee</u>' an <u>a</u>kul <u>ha</u>za
This is too…	هذا…أكثر من اللازم. <u>ha</u>za…<u>ak</u>tar min al-<u>laa</u>zim
– cold/hot	بارد/ساخن <u>baa</u>rid/<u>saa</u>khin
– salty/spicy	مالح/حار <u>maa</u>liH/<u>Haar</u>
– tough/bland	قاسي/عديم النكهة <u>qaa</u>see/'a<u>deem</u> al-<u>nuk</u>-ha
This isn't *clean/fresh*.	هذا ليس نظيف/طازج. <u>ha</u>za <u>lay</u>sa na<u>zeef</u>/<u>taa</u>zij

Paying

The check [bill], please.	الحساب من فضلك. al-<u>Hi</u>saab min <u>fad</u>lak
Separate checks [bills], please.	نريد حساب منفصل لكل شخص من فضلك. nu<u>reed</u> <u>Hi</u>saab mun<u>fa</u>sal li-kul shakhs min <u>fad</u>lak
It's all together.	الحساب يتضمن كل شيء. al-<u>Hi</u>saab yata<u>da</u>man kul shay
Is service included?	هل يتضمن الحساب أجرة الخدمة؟ hal yata<u>da</u>man al-<u>Hi</u>saab <u>uj</u>rat al-<u>khid</u>ma
What's this amount for?	لم هذا المبلغ؟ li<u>maa</u> <u>ha</u>za al-<u>mab</u>lagh

I didn't have that. I had…	أنا لم آخذ هذا. أنا أخذت… <u>ana</u> lam <u>akhuz haza ana akhaz</u>tu…
Can I have *a receipt/an itemized bill*?	أريد إيصال/فاتورة مفصلة. oo<u>reed</u> *ee<u>saal</u>/fa<u>too</u>ra mufa<u>sa</u>la*
That was delicious!	كان الطعام لذيذاً! kaan al-ta<u>'aam</u> la<u>zeez</u>

In restaurants, a 10% tip is fine, although you may want to tip the main waiter and the assistants separately. Make sure you have some small change easily accessible at all times.

Market

| Where are the *carts [trolleys]/baskets*? | أين عربات/سلال التسوق؟ ayn *'ara<u>baat</u>/si<u>laal</u>* al-tasa<u>wooq</u> |
| Where is…? | أين…؟ ayn… |

▶ For food items, see page 84.

I'd like some of *that/this*.	أريد قليلاً من هذا/ذلك. oo<u>reed</u> qa<u>lee</u>lan min *<u>haza</u>/<u>zaa</u>lik*
Can I taste it?	ممكن أتذوق هذا؟ <u>mum</u>kin ata<u>za</u>waq <u>haza</u>
I'd like…	أريد… oo<u>reed</u>…
– a *kilo/half-kilo* of…	كيلو/نصف كيلو… *<u>kee</u>lo/nisf <u>kee</u>lo*…
– a liter of…	ليتر… <u>lee</u>tir…
– a piece of…	قطعة… <u>qit</u>'aat…
– a slice of…	شريحة… sha<u>ree</u>Hat…
More./Less.	أكثر./أقل. *<u>ak</u>tar/<u>aqal</u>*
How much?	كم سعر هذا؟ kam si'r <u>haza</u>
Where do I pay?	أين أدفع؟ ayn adfa'
A bag, please.	كيس من فضلك. kees min <u>fad</u>lak
I'm being helped.	هناك من يساعدني. hu<u>naak</u> man yusaa<u>'id</u>nee

▶ For conversion tables, see page 175.

67

You May Hear...

بم أساعدك؟ bi-maa oo<u>saa</u>'idak	Can I help you?
ماذا تحب؟ <u>maaza</u> tu<u>Hib</u>	What would you like?
هل تريد أي شيء آخر؟ hal tu<u>reed</u> ay shay <u>akh</u>ar	Anything else?
هذا... <u>haza</u>...	That's...

You May See...

يفضل الاستهلاك قبل... yu<u>faddal</u> al-estih<u>laak</u> qabl...	best if used by...
حريرات Huray<u>raat</u>	calories
خال من الدسم khaal min al-dasm	fat free
يحفظ في الثلاجة yu<u>H</u>faz feel ta<u>laaja</u>	keep refrigerated
قد يحتوي على بقايا... qad ya<u>H</u>tawee ala ba<u>qayaa</u>...	may contain traces of...
مناسب للمايكرويف mu<u>naa</u>sib lil-maykro<u>wayf</u>	microwaveable
صالح لغاية... <u>saa</u>leH li-<u>ghaa</u>ya...	sell by...
مناسب للنباتيين mu<u>naa</u>sib lil-nabaatee<u>yeen</u>	suitable for vegetarians

Dishes, Utensils and Kitchen Tools

bottle opener	فتاحة زجاجات fa<u>taa</u>Hat zujaj<u>aat</u>
bowl	زبدية zub<u>dee</u>ya
can opener	فتاحة معلبات fa<u>taa</u>Hat mu'aalab<u>aat</u>
corkscrew	فتاحة نبيذ fa<u>taa</u>Hat na<u>beez</u>
cup	فنجان fin<u>jaan</u>
fork	شوكة <u>shoh</u>ka

frying pan	مقلاة mi<u>ql</u>aah
glass	كأس ka's
(steak) knife	سكين (حادة) si<u>k</u>een (<u>H</u>aada)
measuring cup	فنجان للعيار fin<u>jaa</u>n lil-'aay<u>aar</u>
measuring spoon	ملعقة للعيار <u>mil</u>'aaqa lil-'aay<u>aar</u>
napkin	منديل للمائدة man<u>deel</u> lil-<u>maa</u>'ida
plate	صحن sa<u>H</u>n
pot	وعاء للطبخ wi<u>'aa</u>' lil-tabkh
spatula	ملعقة مسطحة <u>mil</u>'aaqa mu<u>s</u>ata<u>H</u>a
spoon	ملعقة <u>mil</u>'aaqa

Meals

Breakfast

bread	خبز khubz
butter	زبدة <u>zib</u>dah
(cold/hot) cereal	كورن فلكس (بارد/ساخن) korn flayks (<u>baa</u>rid/<u>saa</u>khin)
cheese	جبنة <u>jib</u>nah
coffee/tea...	قهوة/شاي... <u>qah</u>wa/shay...
– black	بدون حليب bi-<u>doo</u>ni <u>H</u>aleeb
– decaf	بدون كافيين bi-<u>doo</u>ni kaa<u>feen</u>
– with milk	مع حليب ma' <u>H</u>aleeb
– with sugar	مع سكر ma' <u>suk</u>kar
– with artificial sweetener	مع مُحلي صناعي ma' <u>muH</u>lee si<u>naa</u>'ee
cold cuts [charcuterie]	لحوم باردة lu<u>Hoom</u> <u>baa</u>rida
croissant	كرواسان krowaa<u>saan</u>

...egg	بيضة... <u>bay</u>da...
– *hard-/soft*-boiled	مسلوقة كثيراً/قليلاً mas<u>loo</u>qa ka<u>tee</u>ran/ qa<u>lee</u>lan
– fried	مقلية mu<u>qlee</u>ya
– scrambled	بيض ممزوج bayd mam<u>zooj</u>
falafel	فلافل fa<u>laa</u>fil
granola [muesli]	ميوزلي m<u>yoo</u>zlee
jam/jelly	مربى/مربى بدون قطع فاكهة mu<u>ra</u>bba/ mu<u>ra</u>bba bi-<u>doo</u>ni qata' <u>faa</u>kiha
...juice	عصير... 'aa<u>seer</u>...
– apple	تفاح tu<u>faaH</u>
– grapefruit	كريب فروت <u>grayp</u>froot
– olive	زيتون zay<u>toon</u>
– orange	برتقال burtu<u>gaal</u>
milk	حليب Ha<u>leeb</u>
muffin	فطيرة حلوى fa<u>tee</u>ra <u>Hel</u>wa
oatmeal	شوفان shoo<u>faan</u>
omelet	عجة <u>ejj</u>a
roll	خبز سمّون khubz sa<u>moon</u>
sausage	سجق <u>suj</u>uq
toast	خبز محمص khubz mu<u>Ham</u>mas
yogurt	لبن labn
water	ماء maa'

I'd like...	أريد... oo<u>reed</u>...
More..., please.	<u>ak</u>tar...min <u>fad</u>lak أكثر...من فضلك.

i A typical Arabic breakfast would consist of tea, fool (mashed broad beans in tahini and yogurt sauce) and falafel (chick pea patty), eggs, olives, cheese and bread. Many hotels will offer this and more Western-style dishes as well. Typically Arab breakfast savories include: لبنة (<u>lab</u>nah) Greek yogurt; مكدوس (mak<u>doos</u>) pickled stuffed eggplants; زيت و زعتر (zayt wa-<u>za</u>'atar) ground thyme and olive oil dip; شنكليش (shank<u>leesh</u>) matured strained yogurt; مسبّحة (mus<u>sa</u>baHa) chickpeas in tahini and yogurt sauce.

Bread

wholewheat [wholemeal] bread	عيش بلدي 'aaysh <u>bala</u>dee
Tunisian semolina bread	خبز مبسس khubz mu<u>bass</u>is
bread browned in the oven	خبز محمص khubz mu<u>Ham</u>mas
Egyptian bread rings covered in sesame seeds	سميط sem<u>ee</u>T

i Bread خبز (khubz) is very important to Arabs and is eaten with every meal. In Egyptian Arabic it is often called عيش ('aaysh), which literally means "life". It is considered disrespectful to throw away bread or drop it on the floor. Traditional Arabic bread is round, flat and only slightly leavened.

With/Without..., please.	مع/بدون....من فضلك. ma'/bi-<u>doo</u>ni...min <u>fad</u>lak
I can't have...	لا أستطيع أن آكل.... laa asta<u>tee</u>'a an <u>aa</u>kul...

Appetizers [Starters]

dip made with eggplant [aubergine] and tahini paste	بابا غنوج babaghannooj
Egyptian smoked gray mullet roe	بطارخ bataarikh
dip made of ground chickpeas and sesame paste	حمص Hummus
white, soft cheese (similar to feta) mashed with tomatoes and herbs	جبنة بيضاء بالطماطم jibna bayda bil-tamaatim
fried or grilled chopped meat patties	كفتة kofta
dip made of sesame paste with olive oil, lemon and cumin, popular in Egypt	طحينة taHeena
vine leaves stuffed with rice and sometimes chopped meat	ورق عنب waraq 'aanab

i Appetizers مازة (mazza) are an important part of an Arabic meal. A mixture of appetizers is usually placed in the middle of the table and shared by everyone.

I'd like...	أريد... ooreed...
More..., please.	أكثر...من فضلك. aktar...min fadlak

Soup

bean soup	شوربة بقول shoorbat buqool
chicken soup	شوربة دجاج shoorbat dujaaj
tomato soup	شوربة طماطم shoorbat tamaatim
vegetable soup	شوربة خضار shoorbat khudaar
thick Egyptian soup made of finely chopped Jew's mallow leaves (similar to spinach), cooked with meat	ملوخية mulookheeya
thick soup made from calves' hooves	شوربة كوارع shoorbat kawaare'a

i Soup is popular in winter and tends to be rich. It can be accompanied by bread and sometimes includes noodles. There is a huge variety of soup based on beans, vegetables and meat.

Fish and Seafood

clam	بطلينوس batleenoos
cod	قد qud
crab	سرطان sartaan
halibut	هلبوت haliboot
herring	رنكة ranka
lobster	كركند karakand
octopus	أخطبوط ukhtuboot
oyster	محار maHaar

With/Without…, please.	مع/بدون.... من فضلك. ma'/bi-dooni…min fadlak
I can't have…	لا أستطيع أن آكل... laa astatee'a an aakul…

salmon	سلمون sal<u>moo</u>n
sea bass	قاروس qaa<u>roo</u>s
shrimp	قريدس qu<u>ray</u>dis
sole	سمك موسى <u>sa</u>mak <u>moo</u>sa
squid	حبّار Hab<u>baa</u>r
swordfish	أبو سيف abu sayf
trout	تروتة <u>troo</u>ta
tuna	طون toon

> *i* In coastal areas, take advantage of the wonderful variety of fresh fish and seafood. You'll find the fish is often laid out fresh on ice or even alive in tanks for you to take your pick. Fish is usually eaten whole, either grilled مشوي (<u>mash</u>wee) or fried مقلي (<u>maq</u>lee), although fish kabobs كباب سمك (ka<u>baa</u>b <u>sa</u>mak) are also popular.

Meat and Poultry

bacon	لحم خنزير مملح laHm khan<u>zee</u>r mu<u>ma</u>llaH
beef	لحم بقري laHm <u>ba</u>qaree
chicken	لحم دجاج laHm du<u>jaa</u>j
duck	لحم بط laHm but
ham	جامبون jaam<u>boo</u>n

rare	نيئ في الوسط nee' feel wast
medium	نصف مطبوخ nisf mat<u>boo</u>kh
well-done	مطبوخ جيداً mat<u>boo</u>kh <u>jay</u>yidan

I'd like...	أريد... oo<u>ree</u>d...
More..., please.	أكثر...من فضلك. <u>ak</u>tar...min <u>fad</u>lak

lamb	لحم غنم laHm <u>gha</u>num
liver	كبد kabd
pork	لحم خنزير laHm khan<u>zeer</u>
rabbit	لحم أرانب laHm a<u>raa</u>nib
sausage	سجق <u>su</u>juk
steak	ستيك steek
turkey	ديك رومي deek <u>roo</u>mee
veal	لحم عجل laHm 'eejl

i

Traditionally "meat" لحم (al-laHm) in the Middle East meant lamb or mutton as cattle was not reared and pork لحم خنزير (laHm al-khan<u>zeer</u>) is forbidden by Islamic law. Although lamb is still probably the most widely available meat, beef is now also popular and chicken, turkey, duck, pigeon and some other small birds are staples of Arabic cuisine. In some areas goat, rabbit and camel meat are eaten. Popular dishes include: كبة نية (kibba <u>nay</u>ya) raw chopped meat with spices; طاجن (<u>taa</u>jin) lamb stew baked in clay pots with fruit and honey, a specialty of North Africa; فتة (<u>fat</u>ta) mutton boiled with rice and bread soaked in broth, vinegar and garlic; كبيبة (ku<u>bay</u>ba) chopped meat and cracked wheat, either in balls or flat in a tray; سليق (sa<u>leeq</u>) lamb cooked in spiced milk and served on rice, a Bedouin specialty; حمام محشي (Ha<u>maam</u> <u>maH</u>shee) pigeon stuffed with cracked wheat or rice.

Vegetables and Staples

| artichoke | أرضي شوكي ardi<u>shoo</u>kee |
| asparagus | هليون hal<u>yoon</u> |

| *With/Without...*, please. | مع/بدون..., من فضلك. ma'/bi-<u>doo</u>ni...min <u>fad</u>lak |
| I can't have... | لا أستطيع أن آكل... laa asta<u>tee</u>'a an <u>aa</u>kul... |

75

avocado	أفكادو	afakaadoo
beans	بقول	buqool
broccoli	بركولي	brookoolee
cabbage	ملفوف	malfoof
carrot	جزر	jizr
chickpea	حمص	Hummus
corn	ذرة	zurra
couscous	كسكس	kuskus
cracked wheat	تبولة	tabboola
eggplant [aubergine]	باذنجان	baazinjaan
garlic	ثوم	soom
green bean	فاصوليا	faasoolya
Jew's mallow (herb)	ملوخية	mulookheeya
lentils	عدس	'aads
lettuce	خس	khas
mushroom	فطر	fitr
okra [ladies' fingers]	بامية	bamya
olive	زيتون	zaytoon
onion	بصل	basal
pasta	معجنات	mu'aajanaat
pea	بازلاء	baazilaa'
pickled vegetables	طرشي	turshee
potato	بطاطس	bataatis
radish	فجل	fajl

I'd like…	أريد…	ooreed…
More…, please.	أكثر…من فضلك.	aktar…min fadlak

76

rice	رز ruz
red/green pepper	فليفلة حمراء/خضراء fu<u>lay</u>fila <u>Ham</u>raa'/<u>khadraa'</u>
tomato	طماطم ta<u>maa</u>tim
spinach	سبانخ sa<u>baa</u>nikh
squash	يقطين yaq<u>teen</u>
tabbouleh (cracked wheat salad with onion, tomato, mint, olive oil and lemon)	تبولة tab<u>boo</u>la
vegetable	خضار khu<u>daar</u>
zucchini [courgette]	كوسا <u>koo</u>sa

Fruit

apple	تفاح tu<u>faaH</u>
apricot	مشمش <u>mish</u>mish
banana	موز mooz
blueberry	عنبية 'aana<u>bee</u>ya
cherry	كرز <u>ka</u>raz
date	تمر <u>ta</u>mar
fig	تين teen
fruit	فاكهة <u>faa</u>kiha
grape	عنب '<u>aa</u>nab
grapefruit	كريب فروت <u>grayp</u>froot
green plum	جانرك <u>jaan</u>rak
guava	جوافة <u>guaa</u>va
lemon	ليمون lay<u>moon</u>

With/Without…, please.	مع/بدون…، من فضلك. ma'/bi-<u>doo</u>ni…min <u>fad</u>lak
I can't have…	لا أستطيع أن آكل… laa asta<u>tee</u>'a an <u>aa</u>kul…

lime	ليم حامض laym <u>H</u>aamid
melon	شمام sha<u>maam</u>
orange	برتقال burtu<u>qaal</u>
peach	دراق da<u>raaq</u>
pear	أجاص a<u>jaas</u>
pineapple	أناناس ana<u>naas</u>
plum	خوخ khookh
raspberry	توت toot
strawberry	فراولة fa<u>raa</u>wala
watermelon	بطيخ ba<u>teekh</u>

Dessert

semolina cake soaked in syrup	بسبوسة bas<u>boo</u>sa
horn-shaped pastries filled with almonds and flavored with orange-flower water, a specialty of North Africa	كعب الغزال <u>k</u>a'ab al-gha<u>zaal</u>
fried dough balls soaked in syrup	لقمة القاضي <u>luq</u>mat al-<u>qaa</u>dee
rice or corn-flour pudding	مهلبية mahla<u>bee</u>ya
pastry filled with nuts and soaked in syrup	قطايف qa<u>taa</u>yif
sweet hot milk pudding with nuts and raisins	أم علي umm '<u>aa</u>lee

i Arab desserts tend to be very sugary, and served in small portions, together with fruit. The most popular desserts are syrupy pastries or milk-based puddings.

I'd like...	أريد... oo<u>reed</u>...
More..., please.	أكثر...من فضلك. <u>ak</u>tar...min <u>fad</u>lak

Drinks

Essential

The *wine list/drink menu*, please.	قائمة النبيذ/قائمة المشروبات، من فضلك. qaa'imat al-nabeez/al-mashroobaat min fadlak
What do you recommend?	بم تنصحني؟ bima tansaHnee
I'd like a *bottle/glass* of *red/white* wine.	أريد زجاجة/كأس نبيذ أحمر/أبيض. ooreed zujaajat/ka'as nabeez aHmar/abyad
The house wine, please.	نبيذ المحل، من فضلك. nabeez al-maHal min fadlak
Another *bottle/glass*, please.	زجاجة/كأس أخرى، من فضلك. zujaaja/ka'as ukhra min fadlak
I'd like a local beer.	أريد بيرة محلية. ooreed beera maHaleeya
Can I buy you a drink?	هل تحب أن تشرب شيء؟ hal tuHib an tashrab shee'
Cheers!	صحة! siHHa
A *coffee/tea*, please.	قهوة/شاي، من فضلك. qahwa/shay min fadlak
Black.	بدون حليب. bi-dooni Haleeb
With...	مع...maa'...
– milk	حليب Haleeb
– sugar	سكر sukkar
– artificial sweetener	مُحلي صناعي muHlee sinaa'ee
A..., please.	... من فضلك. ...min fadlak
– juice	عصير 'aaseer
– soda	صودا sooda
– (sparkling/still) water	مياه (غازية/معدنية) miyaah (ghaazeeya/ ma'adaneeya)
Is the water safe to drink?	هل المياه آمنة للشرب؟ hal al-miyaah aamina lil-shurb

Non-alcoholic Drinks

coffee	قهوة <u>qa</u>hwa
hot chocolate	شراب الشوكلاتة sha<u>raab</u> al-shooka<u>laa</u>ta
juice	عصير 'aa<u>seer</u>
milk	حليب Ha<u>leeb</u>
soda	صودا <u>soo</u>da
(iced) tea	(آيس) تي/شاي (ays) tee/shay
(sparkling/still) water	مياه (غازية/معدنية) mi<u>yaah</u> (ghaa<u>zee</u>ya/ma'ada<u>nee</u>ya)

I'd like...	أريد... oo<u>reed</u>...
Another..., please.	آخر...من فضلك. <u>aa</u>khar...min <u>fad</u>lak

Freshly squeezed juices and bottles of international and local soft drinks are popular throughout the Arab world. You will find juice bars serving a large variety of delicious fruit juices and cocktails squeezed in front of you. Soft drinks often have to be drunk on the spot and the bottles returned. Non-alcoholic beer and wine are also becoming widely available, and there are several international and local brands on the market.

You may also find كركديه (<u>kar</u>kaday), a drink made from the flowers of the fuchsia plant that can be drunk hot or cold, and tamarind عصير تمر هندي ('aa<u>seer</u> tamr <u>hin</u>dee) or sugar-cane juice عصير قصب ('aa<u>seer</u> <u>qa</u>sab).

Tea and coffee are popular throughout the Middle East, drunk both in the traditional way—strong, sweet and black—and increasingly also in the Western style. You can find Western-style cafes within hotels and in the larger towns, or you can try out a local coffee house المقهى (al-<u>maq</u>ha).

Tea is served in a glass, with sugar and sometimes mint. Coffee is served in an espresso-sized glass or cup and is very strong and black. The coffee beans are roasted and cardamom is added for flavoring. You can order it سكر وسط (<u>suk</u>kar <u>wa</u>sat) regular, سكر زيادة (<u>suk</u>kar zi<u>yaa</u>da) extra sweet or سادة (<u>saa</u>da) without sugar.

You can also order a شيشة (<u>shee</u>sha) or نرجيلة (naar<u>jee</u>la), the famous Arab water pipe. You need to specify whether you want تنبك (<u>tan</u>bak), a natural coarse tobacco, or معسّل (mu'<u>aa</u>sal), a lighter tobacco mixed with molasses. You can also play backgammon or dominoes. It's almost exclusively men who patronize coffee houses, and if you go as an unaccompanied woman you might feel ill at ease.

You May Hear...

هل تحب أن تشرب شيء؟ hal tu<u>Hib</u> an <u>ta</u>shrab shee'	Can I get you a drink?
مع حليب أو سكر؟ maa' <u>Ha</u>leeb oh <u>su</u>kkar	With milk or sugar?
مياه غازية أو معدنية؟ mi<u>yaah</u> ghaa<u>zee</u>ya oh ma'ada<u>nee</u>ya	Sparkling or still water?

Aperitifs, Cocktails and Liqueurs

brandy	براندي <u>braan</u>dee
gin	جن jin
rum	رَم rum
scotch	سكوتش skootsh
tequila	تكيلا te<u>kee</u>la
vodka	فودكا <u>voo</u>dka
whisky	وسكي <u>wees</u>kee

i

Alcohol is strictly forbidden to Muslims under Islamic law, and in some Arab countries, notably Saudi Arabia, it is illegal. However, in other Arabic-speaking countries, alcohol can be bought in tourist areas and hotels. Lebanon and Egypt have a long history of wine and beer production, and local brews are worth sampling—and are cheaper than imported brands. A local specialty of Lebanon and the Levant is عرق ('<u>aa</u>raq), an aniseed drink similar to Greek ouzo or French pastis.

I'd like...	أريد.... oo<u>reed</u>...
Another..., please.	آخر....من فضلك. <u>aa</u>khar...min <u>fad</u>lak

Beer

beer	بيرة <u>bee</u>ra
– bottled/draft	زجاجة/حنفية zu<u>jaaj</u>a/Hana<u>fee</u>ya
– dark/light	غامقة/فاتحة <u>ghaa</u>miqa/<u>faa</u>tiHa
– local/imported	محلية/مستوردة maHa<u>lee</u>ya/mus<u>toh</u>rida
– non-alcoholic	بدون كحول bi-<u>doo</u>ni ku<u>Hool</u>

Wine

wine	نبيذ na<u>beez</u>
champagne	شمبانيا sham<u>baan</u>ya
red/white	أحمر/أبيض <u>aH</u>mar/<u>ab</u>yad
house/table	المحل/مائدة al-ma<u>Hal</u>/<u>maa</u>'eda
dry/sweet	مز/حلو mezz/<u>He</u>loo
sparkling	فوار fa<u>waar</u>
dessert wine	نبيذ حلو na<u>beez</u> <u>He</u>loo

شاتوه مزار شاتوه كساری (<u>shaa</u>toh moo<u>saar</u>) Château Musar and (<u>shaa</u>toh ke<u>saar</u>a) Château Ksara are two of the best types of wine available in the Arab world. They are produced in the Bekaa Valley in Lebanon, and have won international awards.

almond	لوز looz
apple	تفاح tuf<u>aa</u>H
apricot	مشمش <u>mish</u>mish
apricot juice	عصير مشمش 'aa<u>seer</u> <u>mish</u>mish
artichoke	أرضي شوكي ardi<u>shoo</u>kee
artificial sweetener	محلي صناعي <u>muH</u>lee si<u>naa</u>'ee
asparagus	هليون hal<u>yoon</u>
avocado	أفكادو afa<u>kaa</u>doo
bacon	لحم خنزير مملح laHm khan<u>zeer</u> mu<u>mall</u>aH
banana	موز mooz
basil	ريحان ree<u>Haan</u>
bass	قاروس qaa<u>roos</u>
bay leaf	غار ghaar

bean soup	شوربة بقول shoorbat buqool
beans	بقول buqool
beef	لحم بقري laHm baqaree
beer	بيرة beera
beet	شوندر shawandar
blueberry	عنبية 'aanabeeya
brain	مخ mukh
brandy	براندي braandee
bread	خبز khubz
breast (of chicken)	سَفن دجاج safan dujaaj
broccoli	بركولي brookoolee
broth	مَرق maraq
brown (fava) beans	فول fool
burger	برغر burghur
butter	زبدة zibda
buttermilk	لبن laban
cabbage	ملفوف malfoof
cake	كعكة ka'aka
camel meat	لحم جمل laHm jamal
candy [sweets]	سكاكر sakaakir
cantaloupe	شمام shammaam
caper	كبر kabar
caramel	كراميل karameel
caraway	كراوية karaawaay
cardamon	حب الهال Habb al-haal
carrot juice	عصير جزر 'aaseer jazar
carrot	جزر jazar

cashew	كاجو kaajoo
cauliflower	نبات الزهرة nabaat al-zahra
celery	كرفس karafs
cereal	كورن فلكس korn flayks
cheese	جبنة jibna
cherry	كرز karaz
chestnut	كستناء kastanaa'
chicken	لحم دجاج laHm dujaaj
chicken soup	شوربة دجاج shoorbat dujaaj
chickpea	حمص Hummus
chili	شطّة shatta
chili pepper	فليفلة حارة fulayfila Haara
chocolate	شوكولاتة shookoolaata
chop	قطعة لحم مع العظم qit'at laHm maa' al-'azm
chopped meat	لحم مقطع laHm muqatta'a
cilantro [coriander]	كزبرة kuzbara
cinnamon	قرفة qirfa
clam	بطلينوس batleenoos
clove	قرنفل qurunfil
coconut	جوز هند jooz hind
cod	قد qud
coffee	قهوة qahwa
cold cuts	لحوم باردة luHoom baarida
cookie [biscuit]	بسكوت baskoot
corn	ذرة zurra
corned beef	لحم عجل معلب laHm 'ajil mu'allab
cornmeal	دقيق قمح daqeeq qamH

couscous	كسكس kuskus
crab	سرطان البحر sartaan al-baHr
crabmeat	لحم سرطان البحر laHm sartaan al-baHr
cracked wheat	برغل burghul
cracker	بسكوت مملح baskoot mumallaH
cranberry	توت برّي toot barree
cream	قشطة qishta
cream (whipped)	كريمة kreema
cream cheese	جبنة للدهن jibna lil-dahn
crème caramel	كريم كراميل kreem karameel
croissant	كرواسان krowaasaan
cucumber	خيار khiyaar
cumin	كمون kammoon
curd cheese	لبنة labna
curd cheese with olive oil	شنكليش shankaleesh
custard	كاسترد kaastard
dates	بلح balaa'
decaf	بدون كافيين bi-dooni kaafeen
dessert wine	نبيذ حلو nabeez Heloo
dill	شبث shibs
dried dates	عجوة 'aajwa
dried melon seeds	بزر بطيخ bizr bateekh
drinks	مشروبات mashroobaat
duck	لحم بط laHm batt
dumpling	زلابية zalaabeeya
eel	أنقليس anqalees
egg	بيضة bayda

egg white	بياض البيضة bayaad al-bayda
egg yolk	صفار البيضة sufaar al-bayda
eggplant [aubergine]	باذنجان baazinjaan
Egyptian bread rings covered in sesame seeds	سميط semeet
endive [chicory]	هندباء hindibaa'
falafel	فلافل falaafil
fava beans	فول مدمس fool mudammis
fennel	شمّار shamaar
feta cheese	جبنة بيضاء jibna baydaa'
fig	تين teen
fish	سمك samak
French fries [chips]	بطاطس مقلية bataatis maqleeya
fritter	فطيرة مقلية fateera maqleeya
fruit	فواكه fawaakih
fruit salad	سلطة فواكه salatat fawaakih
fuchsia tea	كركديه karkadayah
game	لحم طرائد laHm taraa'id
garlic	ثوم soom
garlic sauce	صلصة الثوم salsat al-soom
ghee (clarified butter)	سمنة samna
gherkin	خيار مخلل khiyaar mukhallal
giblet	قلب الطائر qalb al-taa'ir
gin	جِن jin
ginger	زنجبيل zinjibeel
goat	ماعز maa'iz
goat cheese	جبنة ماعز jibnat maa'iz
goose	أوز iwazz

granola [muesli]	myoozlee ميوزلي
grapefruit	graypfroot كريب فروت
grapes	'aanab عنب
green bean	faasoolya فاصوليا
green pepper	fulayfila khadraa' فليفية خضراء
grilled corn	zurra mashweeya ذرة مشوية
ground beef [mince]	laHma mafrooma لحمة مفرومة
guava	gwaava جوافة
guava juice	'aaseer jawaafa عصيرجوافة
haddock	Hadooq حدوق
hake	qadd قد
halibut	haliboot هلبوت
ham	jaamboon جامبون
hamburger	hamboorger همبرغر
hazelnut	bunduq بندق
heart	qalb قلب
hen	dujaaja دجاجة
herb	'ashaba عشبة
herring	ranka رنكة
honey	'asal عسل
hot (spicy)	Haar حار
hot dog	"hot dog" هوت دوغ
hot pepper sauce	salsa Haara صلصة حارة
ice cream	aayis kreem آيس كريم
ice cubes	muka'abaat talj مكعبات، ثلج
instant coffee	neskaafay نسكافيه
jam	murabba مربى

jelly	مربى بدون قطع فاكهة murabba bi-dooni qata' faakiha
juice	عصير 'aaseer
kabob	كباب kabaab
ketchup	كتشب ketchup
kid	لحم الجدي laHm al-jadee
kidney	كلية kilya
kiwi	كيوي keewee
kofta (fried or grilled meatballs)	كفتة kofta
lamb	لحم غنم laHm ghanum
leek	كرّاث kuraas
leg	فخذ fakhz
lemon	ليمون laymoon
lemon juice	عصير ليمون 'aaseer laymoon
lemonade	ليموناضة leemoonaada
lentils	عدس 'aads
lettuce	خس khas
lime	ليم حامض laym Haamid
liqueur	ليكيور leekyoor
liver	كبد kabd
lobster	كركند karakand
loin	خِصى khasee
macaroni	معكرونة ma'akroona
mackerel	إسقمري esqamree
mango	منجا manga
mango juice	عصير منجا 'aaseer manga
margarine	زبدة نباتية zibda nabaateeya
marmalade	مربى برتقال murabba burtuqaal

mashed brown beans	فول fool
matured cheese	جبنة معتّقة jibna qadeema
mayonnaise	مايونيز mayooneez
meat	لحم laHm
melon	شمام shamaam
meringue	ميرنغ meerangh
milk	حليب Haleeb
milk pudding	مهلبية muHallabeeya
milk shake	كوكتيل حليب kookteel Haleeb
mineral water	مياه معدنية miyaah ma'adaneeya
mint	نعناع na'ana'
mint tea	شاي بنعناع shaay bi-na'na'
muffin	فطيرة حلوى fateera Helwa
mullet	سلطان ابراهيم sultaan ebraheem
mushroom	فطر fitr
mussel	بلح البحر balaa' al-baHr
mustard	خردل khardal
mutton	لحم الضأن laHm al-za'n
noodles	نودلز noodelz
nougat	نوغة noogha
nutmeg	جوزة الطيب johzat al-tayyib
nuts	مكسرات mukassaraat
oatmeal	شوفان shoofaan
octopus	أخطبوط ukhtaboot
okra [ladies' fingers]	بامية bamya
okra stewed with lamb knuckles	بامية بالموزة baamya bil-mohza
olive	زيتون zaytoon

olive oil	زيت زيتون zayt zaytoon
omelet	عجة ejja
onion	بصل basal
orange	برتقال burtuqaal
orange juice	عصير برتقال 'aaseer burtuqaal
orange liqueur	ليكيور برتقال leekyoor burtuqaal
oregano	زعتر بري za'atar barree
organ meat [offal]	أحشاء الذبيحة aHshaa' al-zabeeHa
oven-browned bread	خبز محمص khubz muHammas
ox	ثور soor
oxtail	ذيل الثور zayl al-soor
oyster	محار maHaar
pancake	فطير fateer
papaya	بابايا babaaya
paprika	بابريكا baabreeka
parsley	بقدونس baqdoonis
parsnip	جزر أبيض jazar abyad
pasta	معجنات mu'aajanaat
pastry	رقائق العجين raqaa'iq al-'ajeen
pâté	باتيه baatay
peach	درّاق daraaq
peanut	فول سوداني fool soodaanee
pear	أجاص ajaas
pea	بازلاء baazilaa'
pecan	جوز البقان jooz al-baqaan
pepper (seasoning)	فلفل filfil
pepper (vegetable)	فليفلة fulayfila

pheasant	حجل Ha<u>j</u>al
pickle	مخلل mu<u>kh</u>al<u>l</u>al
pie	فطيرة fa<u>tee</u>ra
pigeon	حمام Ha<u>maa</u>m
pineapple	أناناس ana<u>naa</u>s
pineapple juice	عصير أناناس 'aa<u>see</u>r aana<u>naa</u>s
pistachio	فستق <u>fus</u>tuq
pizza	بيتزا <u>beet</u>za
plum	خوخ khookh
pomegranate	رُمان ru<u>maa</u>n
pork	لحم خنزير laHm khan<u>zeer</u>
port	بورت boort
potato	بطاطس ba<u>taa</u>tis
potato chip [crisp]	شبس shibs
poultry	دواجن da<u>waa</u>jin
prickly pear	تين شوكي teen <u>shoh</u>kee
prune	خوخ مجفف khookh mu<u>jaf</u>faf
pumpkin	قرع <u>qa</u>ra'
quail	سُمّاني su<u>maa</u>nee
rabbit	لحم أرانب laHm a<u>raa</u>nib
radish	فجل fajl
raisin	زبيب za<u>beeb</u>
raspberry	توت toot
red cabbage	ملفوف أحمر mal<u>foo</u>f <u>a</u>Hmar
red mullet	سمك بوري <u>sa</u>mak <u>boo</u>ree
red pepper	فليفلة حمراء fu<u>lay</u>fila <u>H</u>amraa'
rhubarb	راوند <u>raa</u>vand

rice	رزّ ruzz
rice pudding	رز بحليب ruzz bi-Ha<u>lee</u>b
roast beef	لحم عجل مشوي laHm <u>'aj</u>il <u>mash</u>wee
roll	خبز سمّون khubz sam<u>moon</u>
rosemary	روز ماري roozmaa<u>ree</u>
rum	رم rum
saffron	زعفران za'af<u>raan</u>
sage	مريمية marya<u>mee</u>ya
salad	سلطة <u>sa</u>lata
salami	سلامي sa<u>laa</u>mee
salmon	سلمون sal<u>moon</u>
salt	ملح malH
sandwich	سندويتش <u>sand</u>witsh
sardine	سردين sar<u>deen</u>
sauce	صلصة <u>sal</u>sa
sausage	سجق <u>su</u>juq
scallion [spring onion]	بصل أخضر <u>ba</u>sal <u>akh</u>dar
scallop	أسقلوب eska<u>loob</u>
scotch	سكوتش s<u>koo</u>tch
sea bass	قاروس qaa<u>roos</u>
seafood	مأكولات بحرية ma'akoo<u>laat</u> baH<u>ree</u>ya
semolina	سميد sa<u>meed</u>
semolina bread (Tunisian)	خبز مبسس khubz mu<u>bas</u>sis
semolina cake	بسبوسة bas<u>boo</u>sa
sesame paste	معجون السمسم ma'a<u>joon</u> al-<u>sim</u>sim

sesame seed	سمسم <u>sim</u>sim
shallot	بصل صغير <u>ba</u>sal sagheer
shank	أعلى الفخذ <u>aa</u>'ala al-fakhz
shellfish	أسماك صدفية as<u>maak</u> sada<u>fee</u>ya
sherry	شري <u>sher</u>ree
shish kabob	كباب ka<u>baab</u>
shoulder	كتف <u>ka</u>tif
shrimp [prawn]	قريدس qu<u>ray</u>dis
sirloin	خاصرة البقرة <u>khaa</u>sira al-<u>baq</u>ra
snack	سناك snaak
soda [soft drink]	كازوز ka<u>zooz</u>
sole	سمك موسى <u>sa</u>mak <u>moo</u>sa
soup	شوربة <u>shoor</u>ba
sour cream	لبن رائب <u>la</u>ban <u>raa</u>'ib
soy [soya]	فول الصويا fool al-<u>soo</u>ya
soy sauce	صلصة فول الصويا <u>sal</u>sat fool al-<u>soo</u>ya
soybean [soya bean]	فول الصويا fool al-<u>soo</u>ya
soymilk [soya milk]	حليب الصويا Ha<u>leeb</u> al-<u>soo</u>ya
spaghetti	سباجتي spaa<u>get</u>tee
spices	توابل ta<u>waa</u>bil
spinach	سبانخ sa<u>baa</u>nikh
spirits	مشروبات كحولية mash<u>roo</u>baat kuHoo<u>lee</u>ya
spit-roasted meat	شاورمة sha<u>war</u>ma
squash	يقطين yaq<u>teen</u>
squid	حبّار Hab<u>baar</u>
steak	ستيك steek

strawberry	فراولة faraawala
strawberry juice	عصير فريز 'aaseer frayz
stuffed vine leaves	ورق عنب waraq 'aanab
sugar	سكر sukkar
sugar-cane juice	عصير قصب 'aaseer qasab
sweet and sour sauce	صوص حلو و حامض soos Helu wa-Haamid
sweet corn	حبوب الذرة Huboob al-zurra
sweet hot milk pudding	أم علي umm 'aalee
sweet pastry	قطايف qataayif
sweet pepper	فليفلة حلوة fulayfila Helwa
sweet potato	بطاطس حلوة bataatis Helwa
sweetener	محلي صناعي muHlee sinaa'ee
swordfish	سمك أبو سيف samak aboo sayf
syrup	قطْر qatr
tahini paste	طحينة taHeena
tamarind juice	عصير تمر هندي 'aaseer tamr hindee
tangerine	يوسفي yoosifee
tarragon	طرخون tarakhoon
tea	شاي shaay
thyme	زعتر za'atar
toast	خبز محمص khubz muHammas
tofu	توفو toofoo
tomato	طماطم tamaatim
tomato soup	شوربة طماطم shoorbat tamaatim
tongue	لسان lisaan
tonic water	مياه تونيك miyaah tooneek

tripe	كرش	karish
trout	تروتة	troota
truffles	كمأة	kam'a
tuna	طون	toon
turkey	ديك رومي	deek roomee
turnip	لفت	lift
vanilla	فانيلا	faaneela
veal	لحم عجل	laHm 'eejl
vegetable	خضار	khudaar
vegetable soup	شوربة خضار	shoorbat khudaar
venison	لحم غزال	laHm ghazaal
vermicelli cake	كنافة	kunaafa
vermouth	فيرموت	feermoot
vine leaves	ورق عنب	waraq 'anab
vinegar	خل	khall
vodka	فودكا	foodka
walnut	جوز	jooz
water	ماء	maa'
watercress	بقلة	baqla
watermelon	بطيخ	batteekh
wheat	قمح	qamH
whisky	ويسكي	weeskee
whole wheat bread [wholemeal bread]	خبز أسمر	'aaysh baladee
wine	نبيذ	nabeet
yogurt	لبن	labn
zucchini [courgette]	كوسا	koosa

▼ *People*

Essential

Hello!	السلام عليكم! al-sa<u>laam</u> 'aa<u>lay</u>kum
Hi!	<u>mar</u>Haban مرحبا!
How are you?	كيف الحال؟ kayf al-Haal
Fine, thanks.	بخير، الحمد لله. bi-khayr al-Hamdul<u>ill</u>ah
Excuse me!	لو سمحت! loh sa<u>ma</u>Ht
Do you speak English?	تتكلم إنكليزي؟ tatak<u>all</u>am engl<u>ee</u>zee
What's your name?	ما اسمك؟ maa <u>es</u>mak
My name is…	اسمي… <u>es</u>mee…
Nice to meet you.	تشرفنا. tashar<u>af</u>na
Where are you from?	من أين أنت؟ min ayn <u>an</u>ta
I'm from the U.S./U.K.	أنا من أمريكا/بريطانيا. ana min am<u>ree</u>ka/bree<u>tan</u>ya
What do you do?	ماذا تعمل؟ <u>maa</u>za <u>ta</u>'aamal
I work for…	أنا أعمل في… <u>a</u>na <u>a</u>'aamal fee…
I'm a student.	أنا طالب♂/طالبة♀. <u>a</u>na <u>taa</u>lib♂/<u>taa</u>liba♀
I'm retired.	أنا متقاعد♂/متقاعدة♀. <u>a</u>na mutaq<u>aa</u>'id♂/mutaq<u>aa</u>'ida♀
Do you like…?	هل تحب…؟ hal tu<u>Hib</u>…
Goodbye.	مع السلامة. ma' al-sal<u>aa</u>ma
See you later.	إلى اللقاء. <u>i</u>lal-liq<u>aa</u>'

Communication Difficulties

Do you speak English?	تتكلم إنكليزي؟ tatakallam engleezee
Does anyone here speak English?	هل يتكلم أحد هنا إنكليزي؟ hal yatakallam aHad huna engleezee
I don't speak (much) Arabic.	أنا لا أتكلم العربية (جيداً). ana laa atakallam al-'aarabeeya (jayidan)
Can you speak more slowly?	ممكن تتكلم ببطء؟ mumkin tatakallam bi-but'
Can you repeat that?	ممكن تعيد؟ mumkin tu'eed
Excuse me?	عفواً؟ afwan
What was that?	ماذا قلت؟ maaza qulta
Can you spell it?	كيف تُكتب؟ kayf tuktab
Please write it down.	اكتبها من فضلك. uktubha min fadlak
Can you translate this into English for me?	ممكن تترجم لي هذا إلى الانكليزي؟ mumkin tutarjim lee haza ila-engleezee
What does *this/that* mean?	ماذا يعني هذا/ذاك؟ maaza ya'anee haza/zaalik
I understand.	فهمت. fahimtu
I don't understand.	لا أفهم. laa afham
Do you understand?	هل تفهم؟ hal tafham

You May Hear...

أنا لا أتكلم إنكليزي جيداً. <u>a</u>na laa atakallam engl<u>ee</u>zee j<u>a</u>yidan

I only speak a little English.

أنا لا أتكلم إنكليزي. <u>a</u>na laa atakallam engl<u>ee</u>zee

I don't speak English.

Making Friends

Hello!	السلام عليكم! al-sal<u>aa</u>m 'aal<u>a</u>ykum
Hi!	مرحبا <u>mar</u>Haban
Good morning.	صباح الخير. sab<u>aa</u>H al-khayr
Good afternoon.	مساء الخير. mas<u>aa</u>' al-khayr
Good evening.	مساء الخير. mas<u>aa</u>' al-khayr
My name is...	اسمي... <u>e</u>smoo...
What's your name?	ما اسمك؟ maa <u>e</u>smak
I'd like to introduce you to...	أحب أن أعرفك على... u<u>Hib</u> an u'arifak 'ala...

Pleased to meet you.	تشرفنا. tasha<u>raf</u>na
How are you?	كيف الحال؟ kayf al-Haal
Fine, thanks. And you?	بخير، الحمد لله. و أنت؟ bi-khayr al-Hamdu<u>lil</u>lah wa <u>an</u>ta

---

i Arabic speakers usually have three names: their own first name, their father's first name and their family or last name. For example, the son of Mohammed Yousef Shaheen would be Ashraf Mohammed Shaheen. To be less formal, drop the middle name: Mohammed Shaheen/Ashraf Shaheen. Note that this also applies to women, who retain their family name after marriage rather than adopting their husband's. So, the daughter of Mohammed Yousef Shaheen would be Mona Mohammed Shaheen.

---

i There are many different greetings in Arabic depending on the situation. As a tourist it is better to stick to one of the general greetings, such as السلام عليكم (al-sa<u>laam</u> aalaykum) hello or مرحبا (<u>mar</u>Haban) hi. It's also customary to shake hands when you meet someone.

Travel Talk

I'm here…	أنا هنا... <u>a</u>na <u>hu</u>na…
– on business	في رحلة عمل fee <u>riH</u>lat 'aamal
– on vacation [holiday]	في إجازة fee e<u>jaa</u>za
– studying	للدراسة lil-di<u>raa</u>sa
I'm staying for…	أنا هنا لمدة... <u>a</u>na <u>hu</u>na li-<u>mu</u>dat…
I've been here…	أنا هنا منذ.... <u>a</u>na <u>hu</u>na <u>mun</u>zu…
– a day	يوم yohm
– a week	أسبوع us<u>boo</u>'
– a month	شهر shahr

102

▶ For numbers, see page 168.

Where are you from?	من أين أنت؟ min ayn <u>an</u>ta
I'm from…	أنا من… <u>a</u>na min…
Have you ever been to…?	زرت…بحياتك؟ <u>zu</u>rta…bi-Ha<u>yaa</u>tak
– Australia	أستراليا ost<u>raa</u>leeya
– Canada	كندا <u>ka</u>nada
– Ireland	أيرلندا ir<u>lan</u>da
– the U.K.	بريطانيا bri<u>taa</u>neeya
– the U.S.	أمريكا am<u>ree</u>ka

Relationships

Who are you with?	مع من أنت؟ ma' man <u>an</u>ta
I'm here alone.	أنا هنا وحدي. <u>a</u>na <u>hu</u>na <u>waH</u>dee
I'm with my…	أنا مع… <u>a</u>na ma'…
– husband/wife	زوجي/زوجتي <u>zoh</u>jee/<u>zoh</u>jatee
– boyfriend/girlfriend	صاحبي/صاحبتي <u>saa</u>Hibee/ saa<u>hi</u>batee
– friend/friends	صديق/أصدقاء sa<u>deeq</u>/asdi<u>qaa</u>'
– colleague/colleagues	زميل/زملاء za<u>meel</u>/zuma<u>laa</u>'
When's your birthday?	متى عيد ميلادك؟ <u>ma</u>ta a'eed mee<u>laa</u>dak
How old are you?	كم عمرك؟ kam '<u>um</u>ruk
I'm…	عمري… '<u>um</u>ree…

▶ For numbers, see page 168.

Are you married?	هل أنت متزوج؟♂/هل أنت متزوجة؟♀ hal <u>an</u>ta muta<u>za</u>wij ♂/hal <u>an</u>ti muta<u>za</u>wija ♀

I'm...	...أنا... ana...
– single	'aazib ♂/'aaziba ♀ عازب ♂/عازبة ♀
– in a relationship	murtabit ♂/murtabita ♀ مرتبط ♂/مرتبطة ♀
– engaged	khaatib ♂/makhtooba ♀ خاطب ♂/مخطوبة ♀
– married	mutazawij ♂/mutazawija ♀ متزوج ♂/متزوجة ♀
– divorced	mutalaq ♂/mutalaqa ♀ مطلق ♂/مطلقة ♀
– separated	munfasil ♂/munfasila ♀ منفصل ♂/منفصلة ♀
– widowed	armal ♂/armala ♀ أرمل ♂/أرملة ♀
Do you have *children/ grandchildren*?	'aandak atfaal/aHfaad عندك أطفال/أحفاد؟

Work and School

What do you do?	bi-maaza ta'amal بماذا تعمل؟
What are you studying?	maaza tadrus ماذا تدرس؟
I'm studying...	ana adrus... أنا أدرس...
I...	ana... أنا...
– am a consultant	mustashaar ♂/ mustashaara ♀ مستشار ♂/مستشارة ♀
– am unemployed	ghayr muwazzaf ♂/ghayr muwazzafa ♀ غير موظف ♂/غير موظفة ♀
– work at home	aa'amal feel bayt أعمل في البيت
Who do you work for?	li-Hisaabi man ta'amal لحساب من تعمل؟
I work for...	aa'amal li-Hisaabi... أعمل لحساب...

►For business travel, see page 141.

Weather

What's the forecast?	ma hiya tawaqoo'aat al-taqs ما هي توقعات الطقس؟
What *beautiful/terrible* weather!	al-taqs raa'ia/sayee' jidan الطقس رائع/سيئ جداً!

It's...	...الطقس al-taqs...
– cool/warm	بارد قليلاً/دافئ baarid qaleelan/daafi'
– cold/hot	بارد/حار baarid/Haar
– rainy/sunny	ممطر/مشمس mumtir/mushamis
Do I need *a jacket/an umbrella*?	هل أحتاج جاكيت/مظلة؟ hal aHtaaj *jakeet/mizalla*

▶ For temperature, see page 176.

Romance

Essential

Would you like to go out for *a drink/dinner*?	هل تريد الذهاب إلى البار/لتناول العشاء؟ hal tureed al-zahaab *ilal-baar/ li-tanawool al-'aashaa'*
What are your plans for *tonight/tomorrow*?	ما خطتك لليلة/للغد؟ maa khututak *lil-layla/lil-ghad*
Can I have your number?	ممكن آخذ رقمك؟ mumkin aakhuz raqmak
Can I join you?	ممكن أنضم لك؟ mumkin andam lak
Can I get you a drink?	هل تحب أن تشرب شيء؟ hal tuHib an tashrab shay
I like you. (*said to a woman by a man*)	أنا معجب بكِ. ana mu'ajab beeki
(*said to a man by a woman*)	أنا معجبة بك. ana mu'ajaba beeka
I love you. (*said to a woman by a man*)	أنا أحبكِ. ana uHibbuki
(*said to a man by a woman*)	أنا أحبك. ana uHibbuka

For simplicity, only forms used to address a man have been included, except where indicated. For female form, see page 166.

Making Plans

Would you like to go out for coffee?

هل تحب أن نذهب لشرب القهوة؟
hal tuHibb an taz-hab li-shurb al-qahwa

What are your plans for…?

ما خططك لـ...؟ maa khututak li-…

– today

اليوم al-yohm

– tonight

الليلة lil-layla

– tomorrow

الغد al-ghad

– this weekend

عطلة نهاية الأسبوع 'utlat nihaayat al-'usboo'

Where would you like to go?

أين تحب أن تذهب؟ ayn tuHib an taz-hab

I'd like to go to…

أريد أن أذهب إلى... ooreed an az-hab ila…

Do you like…?

هل تحب...؟ hal tuHib…

Can I have your number/
e-mail?

ممكن آخذ رقم تلفونك/عنوانك الالكتروني؟
mumkin aakhuz raqmak/'unwaanak al-elektroonee

▶ For e-mail and phone, see page 50.

LEARN THESE! -HAYNICZ

Pick-up [Chat-up] Lines

Can I join you? ممكن أنضم لك؟ <u>mum</u>kin <u>an</u>dam lak

You're very attractive. أنت جذاب جداً. <u>an</u>ta ja<u>zaab</u> <u>jid</u>dan

Let's go somewhere quieter. خلينا نذهب إلى مكان أهدأ. kha<u>lay</u>na <u>naz</u>-hab ila ma<u>kaan</u> <u>ah</u>da'

Accepting and Rejecting

I'd love to. يسرني ذلك. ya<u>sir</u>nee <u>zaa</u>lik

Where should we meet? أين نلتقي؟ ayn nal<u>ta</u>qee

I'll meet you at *the bar/ your hotel*. ألاقيك في البار/فندقك. u<u>laa</u>qeek *feel-baar/fee <u>fun</u>dukik*

I'll come by at… سآتي في الساعة… sa-<u>a</u>tee feel-<u>saa</u>'aa…

What is your address? ما عنوانك؟ maa 'un<u>waa</u>nak

I'm busy. أنا مشغول♂/مشغولة♀. <u>a</u>na mash<u>ghool</u>♂/mash<u>ghoo</u>la♀

I'm not interested. لست مهتماً. <u>las</u>tu muh<u>tam</u>man

Leave me alone. اتركني وحدي. ut<u>ruk</u>nee <u>waH</u>dee

Stop bothering me! توقف عن إزعاجي! ta<u>waq</u>qaf 'an ez<u>'aa</u>jee

Getting Physical

Can I *hug/ kiss* you? ممكن أعانقك/أبوسك؟ <u>mum</u>kin *a<u>boo</u>sak/<u>mum</u>kin u<u>'aa</u>niqak*

Yes. نعم. na'am

No. لا. laa

Stop! توقف! ta<u>waq</u>qaf

Sexual Preferences

١٠١

I'm… أنا… <u>a</u>na…

– heterosexual مغاير الجنس mu<u>ghaa</u>yer al-jins

– gay مثلي الجنس <u>mis</u>lee al-jins

– bisexual مزدوج الجنس muz<u>daw</u>waj al-jins

▼ Fun

Sightseeing

Essential

Where's the tourist information office?	أين مكتب الاستعلامات السياحية؟ ayn maktab al-este'alamaat al-seeyaaHeeya
What are the main attractions?	ما هي المعالم الرئيسية؟ maa hiya al-ma'aalim al-ra'eeseeya
Do you have tours in English?	عندكم جولات سياحية بالإنكليزي؟ 'andakum johlaat seeyaaHeeya bil-engleezee
Can I have a *map/ guide*?	ممكن تعطيني خريطة/كتاب عن المكان؟ mumkin tu'ateenee *khareeta/kitaab* 'an al-makaan

Tourist Information Office

Do you have information on…?	عندكم معلومات عن…؟ 'aandakum ma'aloomaat 'an…
Can you recommend…?	ممكن تنصحني بـ…؟ mumkin tansaHnee bi…
– a bus tour	جولة بالباص johla bil-baas
– an excursion to…	رحلة إلى… riHla ila…
– a sightseeing tour	جولة لزيارة المعالم johla li-ziyaarat al-ma'aalim

> *i* In major tourist areas you will likely find tourist offices مكتب السياحة (maktab al-siyaaHa) downtown with information about attractions, special events, etc. You may also be able to arrange special tours, for example of pharaonic sites or crusader castles, with English-speaking guides.

Tours

I'd like to go on the tour to…	‫أريد أن أذهب في جولة إلى...‬ ooreed an az-hab fee johla ila…
When's the next tour?	‫متى الجولة القادمة؟‬ mata al-johla al-qaadima
Are there tours in English?	‫هل هناك جولات بالإنكليزي؟‬ hal hunaak johlaat bil-engleezee
Is there an English *guide book/audio guide*?	‫هل هناك كتاب/دليل مسجل عن المكان بالإنكليزي؟‬ hal hunaak kitaab/daleel musajjal 'an al-makaan bil-engleezee
What time do we *leave/return*?	‫متى ننطلق/نعود؟‬ mata nantaliq/na'ood
We'd like to see…	‫نريد أن نرى...‬ nureed an nara…
Can we stop here…?	‫ممكن نتوقف هنا...؟‬ mumkin natawaqqaf huna…
– to take photos	‫للتصوير‬ lil-tasweer
– for souvenirs	‫لشراء الهدايا التذكارية‬ li-shiraa' al-hadaaya al-tizkaareeya
– for the restrooms [toilets]	‫للذهاب إلى التواليت‬ lil-zihaab ilal-toowaaleet
Can we look around?	‫ممكن نتفرج؟‬ mumkin natafarraj
Is it handicapped [disabled]-accessible?	‫هل المكان مجهز لاستقبال المعاقين؟‬ hal al-makaan mujahhaz li-esteqbaal al-mu'aaqeen

▶For ticketing, see page 19.

Sights

Where's the…?	‫أين...؟‬ ayn…
– botanical garden	‫حديقة النباتات‬ Hadeeqat al-nabataat
– castle	‫القلعة‬ al-qal'a

– downtown area	مركز المدينة <u>mar</u>kaz al-ma<u>dee</u>na
– library	المكتبة al-<u>mak</u>taba
– market	السوق al-sooq
– museum	المتحف al-<u>mat</u>-Haf
– old town	المدينة القديمة al-ma<u>dee</u>na al-qa<u>dee</u>ma
– palace	القصر al-qasr
– park	الحديقة العامة al-Ha<u>dee</u>qa al-'<u>aa</u>ma
– parliament building	مبنى البرلمان <u>mab</u>na al-barla<u>maan</u>
– ruins	الآثار al-aa<u>saar</u>
– shopping area	منطقة التسوق <u>man</u>taqat al-tasa<u>wooq</u>
– town hall	البلدية al-bala<u>dee</u>ya
– town square	ساحة المدينة <u>saa</u>Hat al-ma<u>dee</u>na
Can you show me on the map?	ممكن تريني على الخريطة؟ <u>mum</u>kin tu<u>ree</u>nee 'alal-kha<u>ree</u>ta

▶ For directions, see page 34.

111

Some of the sightseeing highlights of a region rich in history and architecture include:

Egypt: Pyramids at Giza; Islamic Cairo; Coptic Christian Cairo; Egyptian Museum; pharaonic temples and tombs at Luxor, Aswan and Abu Simbel; Mount Sinai and St. Catherine's Monastery in Sinai

Lebanon: Ruined Roman temple at Ba'albek; Saladin's restored palace at Al-Shouf; Biblical cedar tree forests near Bisherri

Jordan: Ruined Nabataean capital at Petra; Roman amphitheater in Amman

Syria: Medieval crusader castles; Islamic architecture of Damascus and Aleppo; Roman ruins at Palmyra

Saudi Arabia: Ancient Islamic cities of Mecca and Medina (accessible only to Muslims); Nabataean ruins of Mada' in Salih in the north of the country; ruins of original Saudi capital city of al-Dir'iyah near Riyadh

Other countries: Old walled city of Sana'a, Yemen; medieval forts built by local rulers and Portuguese merchant-adventurers in Oman and Bahrain; "Queen of Sheba's palace" ancient ruins and fortifications at Ras al-Khaima in the United Arab Emirates

Impressions

It's…	...إنه... innahu...
– amazing	مدهش mudhish
– beautiful	جميل jameel
– boring	ممل mumill
– interesting	مثير للاهتمام museer lil-ehtimaam

– magnificent	جميل جداً jameel jiddan
– romantic	رومانسي roomaansee
– strange	غريب ghareeb
– stunning	مذهل muz-hil
– terrible	فظيع fazee'a
– ugly	بشع bashe'a
I (don't) like it.	(لا) أحبه. (laa) uHibhu

Religion

Where's the...?	أين... ayn...
– *Catholic/Protestant* church	الكنيسة الكاثوليكية/البروتستانتية al-kaneesa al-katuuleekeeya/ al-brooteestaanteeya
– mosque	الجامع al-jaame'a
– shrine	المزار al-mazaar
– temple	المعبد al-ma'abad
What time is *mass/ the service?*	متى يقام القداس/تقام الصلاة؟ mata yuqaam al-qudaas/tuqaam al-salaat

The Arab world is predominantly Muslim. However, other religions are represented as well—there are large Christian populations in Lebanon and Egypt. Muslims pray five times a day and gather in mosques for Friday prayers. In some areas, non-Muslims may not be able to enter mosques; ask for permission first. If allowed, you should remove your shoes, cover your legs and arms and women should cover their hair.

Shopping

Essential

Where's the *market/mall [shopping centre]*?	أين السوق/المركز التجاري؟ ayn al-sooq/al-markaz al-tijaaree
I'm just looking.	أنا أتفرج فقط. ana atafaraj faqat
Can you help me?	ممكن تساعدني؟ mumkin tusaa'idnee
I'm being helped.	هناك من يساعدني. hunaak man yusaa'idnee
How much?	كم سعره؟ kam si'rhu
That one, please.	ذلك من فضلك. zaalik min fadlak
That's all.	هذا كل شيء. haaza kul shay
Where can I pay?	أين أدفع؟ ayn adfa'
I'll pay *in cash/by credit card*.	سأدفع كاش/ببطاقة الائتمان. sa-adfa' kaash/bi-bitaaqat al-e'atimaan
A receipt, please.	إيصال من فضلك. eesaal min fadlak

Stores

Where's...?	أين... ayn...
– the antiques store	محل الأنتيكات maHal al-antikaat
– the bakery	المخبز al-makhbaz
– the bank	البنك al-bank
– the bookstore	المكتبة al-maktaba
– the camera store	محل الكاميرات maHal al-kameeraat

– the clothing store	محل الملابس maHal al-malaabis
– the gift shop	محل الهدايا التذكارية maHal al-hadaaya al-tizkaareeya
– the health food store	محل الأطعمة الصحية maHal al-aṭ'ima al-siheeya
– the jeweler	محل المجوهرات maHal al-mujoharaat
– the liquor store [off-licence]	محل المشروبات الكحولية maHal al-mashroobaat al-kuHooleeya
– the market	السوق al-sooq
– the music [CD] store	محل السيديات maHal al-seedeeyaat
– the pastry shop	محل الحلويات maHal al-Helweeyaat
– the pharmacy [chemist]	الصيدلية al-saydaleeya
– the produce [grocery] store	محل الخضار maHal al-khuḍaar
– the shoe store	محل الأحذية maHal al-aHzeeya
– the souvenir store	محل الهدايا التذكارية maHal al-hadaaya al-tizkaareeya
– the supermarket	السوبر ماركت al-soopermarkit
– the tobacconist	كشك الجرائد kushk al-jaraa'id
– the toy store	محل ألعاب الأطفال maHal al'aab al-atfaal

Opening hours for stores and banks vary from country to country. Often, stores will close in the middle of the day and re-open later in the afternoon. Times also vary seasonally and particularly during Ramadan (see page 174). Friday is usually the official closing day in the Muslim world, but in some areas this can extend to Saturday as well. Stores and offices will be closed on Sundays in predominantly Christian areas.

Services

Can you recommend...?	ممكن تنصحني بـ...؟ <u>mum</u>kin tan<u>saH</u>nee bi-...
– a barber	حلاق رجالي <u>Halaaq</u> ri<u>jaa</u>lee
– a dry cleaner	محل تنظيف ألبسة ma<u>Hal</u> tan<u>zeef</u> <u>al</u>bisa
– a hairstylist	كوافير koowaa<u>feer</u>
– a laundromat [launderette]	محل تنظيف ألبسة بخدمة ذاتية ma<u>Hal</u> tan<u>zeef</u> <u>al</u>bisa bi-<u>khid</u>ma zaa<u>tee</u>ya
– a nail salon	صالون تجميل sa<u>loon</u> taj<u>meel</u>

– a spa	سبا spa
– a travel agency	<u>mak</u>tab مكتب سياحة و سفر see<u>yaa</u>Ha wa <u>sa</u>far
Can you...this?	<u>mum</u>kin...<u>haa</u>za ممكن...هذا؟
– alter	tu<u>'ad</u>del تعدل
– clean	tu<u>naz</u>zif تنظف
– fix [mend]	tu<u>sal</u>liH تصلح
– press	<u>tik</u>bis تكبس
When will it be ready?	<u>ma</u>ta ya<u>koon</u> متى يكون جاهز؟ <u>jaa</u>hiz

Spa

I'd like...	oo<u>reed</u>... ...أريد
– an *eyebrow/bikini* wax	<u>sha</u>ma' شمع حواجب/خط البيكيني *Ha<u>waa</u>jib/khat al-bee<u>kee</u>nee*
– a facial	tan<u>zeef</u> al-<u>wa</u>jah تنظيف الوجه
– a *manicure/pedicure*	manee<u>koor</u>/ منيكور/بديكور bedee<u>koor</u>
– a massage	ma<u>saaj</u> مساج
Do you...?	hal... هل...؟
– do acupuncture	tuj<u>roon</u> 'e<u>laaj</u> تجرون علاج بالإبر bil-<u>ib</u>ar
– do aromatherapy	tuj<u>roon</u> 'e<u>laaj</u> تجرون علاج أروماتي aroo<u>maa</u>tee
– have oxygen treatment	<u>aan</u>dakum' لديكم علاج بالأوكسجين 'e<u>laaj</u> bil-ohk<u>see</u>jeen
– have a sauna	<u>aan</u>dakum saa<u>oh</u>na' لديكم سونا

Hair Salon

I'd like…   أُريد… ooreed…

– an appointment for   موعد لليوم/للغد moh'id lil-yohm/
  today/tomorrow   lil-ghad

– some color/highlights   صبغة/هاي لايت sabgha/haay laayt

– my hair styled/blow-dried   تسريحة/سشوار tasreeHa/sishwaar

– a haircut   قصة شعر qassat sha'ar

– a trim   تطريف شعر tatreef sha'ar

Not too short.   ليس قصير جداً. laysa qaseer jiddan

Shorter here.   أقصر هنا. aqsar huna

Sales Help ────────────────────

When do you open/   متى تفتحون/تغلقون؟ mata taftaHoon/
close?   taghliqoon

Where's…?   أين…؟ ayn…

– the cashier   المحاسب al-muHaasib

– the escalator   السلالم الكهربائية al-salaalim
                                       al-kahrabaa'eeya

– the elevator [lift]   المصعد al-mis'ad

– the fitting room   غرفة القياس ghurfat al-qeeyaas

– the store directory   دليل المحلات التجارية daleel
                                       al-maHalaat al-tijaareeya

Can you help me?   ممكن تساعدني؟ mumkin
                                       tusaa'idnee

I'm just looking.   أنا أتفرج فقط. ana atafaraj
                                       faqat

I'm being helped.   هناك من يساعدني. hunaak man
                                       yusaa'idnee

Do you have…?   عندكم…؟ 'aandakum…

Can you show me…? | <u>mum</u>kin tu<u>ree</u>nee… ممكن تريني…؟
Can you *ship/wrap* it? | <u>mum</u>kin tur<u>sil</u>hu bil-ba<u>reed</u>/ta<u>liff</u>hu ممكن ترسله بالبريد/تلفه؟

How much? | kam <u>si</u>'rhu كم سعره؟
That's all. | <u>haa</u>za kul shay هذا كل شيء.

▶ For clothing items, see page 125.
▶ For food items, see page 84.
▶ For souvenirs, see page 123.

You May Hear...

<u>mum</u>kin usaa<u>'i</u>dak ممكن أساعدك؟ | Can I help you?
<u>laH</u>za لحظة. | One moment.
<u>maa</u>za tu<u>reed</u> ماذا تريد؟ | What would you like?
ay shay <u>aa</u>khar أي شيء أخر؟ | Anything else?

You May See...

maf<u>tooH</u> مفتوح | open
<u>mugh</u>laq مغلق | closed
<u>mugh</u>laq li-<u>fat</u>rat al-gha<u>zaa</u>' مغلق لفترة الغذاء | closed for lunch
<u>ghur</u>fat al-qee<u>yaas</u> غرفة القياس | fitting room
al-mu<u>Haa</u>sib المحاسب | cashier
kash <u>faqat</u> كاش فقط | cash only
<u>tuq</u>bal bitaa<u>qaat</u> al-e'ti<u>maan</u> تُقبل بطاقات الائتمان | credit cards accepted
oh<u>qaat</u> al-'amal أوقات العمل | business hours
<u>makh</u>raj مخرج | exit

119

Preferences

I'd like something…	...أريد شيء ooreed shay…
– cheap/expensive	رخيص/غالي rakhees/ghaalee
– larger/smaller	أكبر/أصغر akbar/asghar
– nicer	أجمل ajmal
– from this region	من هذه المنطقة min haazih al-mantiqa

Around…	في حدود... fee Hudood…
Is it real?	هل هو أصلي؟ hal huwa aslee
Can you show me *this/ that*?	ممكن تريني هذا/ذلك؟ mumkin tureenee *haaza/zaalik*

Decisions

That's not quite what I want.	هذا ليس بالضبط ما أريد. haaza laysa bil-dabt ma ooreed
No, I don't like it.	لا، لا يعجبني. laa laa yu'ajibnee
It's too expensive.	إنه غالٍ جداً. inahu ghaalee jiddan
I have to think about it.	لازم أفكر في الموضوع. laazim ufakkir feel-mohdoo'
I'll take it.	سآخذه. sa-'aakhuzhu

Bargaining

That's too much.	هذا كثير. haaza kateer
I'll give you…	...سأعطيك sa-'ooteek…
I have only…	...عندي فقط 'aandee faqat…
Is that your best price?	هذا أحسن سعر عندك؟ haaza aHsan si'r 'aandak
Can you give me a discount?	ممكن تعمل لي خصم؟ mumkin ta'amal lee khasm

Although there are large shopping malls and supermarkets in the region, the most interesting way to shop is still in the many local markets سوق (sooq). These sell everything from perfumes and spices to gold and carpets. You will be expected to bargain, but be careful not to overdo it by making an insulting offer.

Paying

How much?	كم سعره؟ kam <u>si</u>'rhu
I'll pay...	سأدفع... sa-<u>a</u>dfa'...
– in cash	كاش. kash
– by credit card	ببطاقة الائتمان bi-bi<u>t</u>aaqat al-e'ati<u>maan</u>
– by traveler's check [cheque]	بشيك سياحي bi-sheek seeyaaHee
Can I use this...card?	ممكن أستخدم هذه البطاقة...؟ <u>mum</u>kin as<u>takh</u>dim <u>haa</u>zih al-bi<u>t</u>aaqat...
– ATM	الصراف الآلي al-sa<u>raaf</u> al-<u>aa</u>lee
– credit	ائتمان e'ati<u>maan</u>
– debit	سحب من الحساب الجاري saHb min al-Hi<u>saab</u> al-<u>jaa</u>ree
How do I use this machine?	كيف استخدم هذه الآلة؟ kayf as<u>takh</u>dim <u>haa</u>zih al-<u>aa</u>la
A receipt, please.	إيصال من فضلك. ee<u>saal</u> min <u>fad</u>lak

 Credit and debit cards are generally accepted in most big cities. However, make sure you always have cash on hand, as cards may not be accepted in traditional shops and markets.

You May Hear...

كيف ستدفع؟ kayf sa-<u>a</u>dfa'	How are you paying?
بطاقة ائتمانك رُفضت. bi<u>taa</u>qat e'ati<u>maa</u>nak <u>ru</u>fidat	Your credit card has been declined.
هويتك الشخصية من فضلك. ha<u>wee</u>yatak al-shakh<u>see</u>ya min <u>fad</u>lak	ID, please.
لا نقبل بطاقات الائتمان. laa <u>naq</u>bal bi<u>taa</u>qaat al-e'ati<u>maan</u>	We don't accept credit cards.
كاش فقط من فضلك. kaash <u>fa</u>qat min <u>fad</u>lak	Cash only, please.
عندك صرافة/أوراق نقدية من الفئات الصغيرة؟ 'aandakum sa<u>raa</u>fa/oh<u>raaq</u> naq<u>dee</u>ya min al-fi'<u>aat</u> al-sa<u>ghee</u>rah	Do you have change/small bills [notes]?

Complaints

I'd like...	أريد... oo<u>reed</u>...
– to exchange this	أن أبدل هذا an u<u>bad</u>dil <u>haa</u>za
– a refund	أن أسترد نقودي an as<u>ta</u>rid nu<u>goo</u>dee
– to see the manager	أن أتكلم مع المدير an ata<u>ka</u>llam ma' al-mu<u>deer</u>

i
Souvenirs can be found at the local markets سوق (sooq), which offer a huge range of interesting articles. You will need to bargain, but try to find out price ranges before you go so you have an idea of what you should be paying. Gold is generally a lot cheaper in the Arab world. Markets may be the best place to buy gold and silver jewelry, especially if you are looking for traditional designs. Items are usually priced by gram weight.

Souvenirs

book	كتاب ki<u>taab</u>
box of chocolates	علبة شوكلاتة '<u>ul</u>bat shookoo<u>laa</u>ta
doll	دمية <u>dum</u>ya
key ring	حمالة مفاتيح Ha<u>maa</u>lat mafaa<u>teeH</u>
postcard	كرت بوستال kart boos<u>taal</u>
pottery	إناء فخاري '<u>enaa</u>' fak<u>haa</u>ree
robe	جلابية jalaa<u>bee</u>ya
rugs	سجاد si<u>jaad</u>
T shirt	تي شيرت tee sheert
toy	لعبة أطفال <u>lu</u>'abat at<u>faal</u>
traditional coffee pot	دلة قهوة تقليدية <u>dal</u>lat <u>qah</u>wa taqlee<u>dee</u>ya

Can I see *this/that*?	ممكن أشوف هذا/ذلك؟ <u>mum</u>kin a<u>shoof</u> <u>haa</u>za/<u>zaa</u>lik
It's in the *window/ display case*.	هو في واجهة المحل/الفترينا. <u>hu</u>wa fee <u>waa</u>jihat al-ma<u>Hal</u>/al-fi<u>tree</u>na
I'd like…	أريد… oo<u>reed</u>…
– a battery	بطارية bataa<u>ree</u>ya
– a bracelet	سوار si<u>waar</u>
– a brooch	بروش broosh
– a clock	ساعة حائطية <u>saa</u>'a <u>Haa</u>'i<u>tee</u>ya
– earrings	حلق <u>Ha</u>laq
– a necklace	عقد 'uqd
– a ring	خاتم <u>khaa</u>tim
– a watch	ساعة يد <u>saa</u>'at yad
I'd like…	أريد… oo<u>reed</u>…
– copper	نحاس nu<u>Haas</u>
– crystal	كريستال krees<u>taal</u>
– diamonds	ألماس al<u>maas</u>
– *white/yellow* gold	ذهب أبيض/أصفر <u>za</u>hab *<u>ab</u>yad/<u>as</u>far*
– pearls	لؤلؤ <u>loo</u>'loo'
– pewter	قصدير qas<u>deer</u>
– platinum	بلاتين blaa<u>teen</u>
– sterling silver	فضة <u>fid</u>da
Is this real?	هل هذا حقيقي؟ hal <u>hu</u>wa Ha<u>qee</u>qee
Can you engrave it?	ممكن تنقش عليه؟ <u>mum</u>kin tu<u>nqush</u> a<u>lay</u>hi

Antiques

How old is it?	ما عمره؟ maa 'umruhu
Do you have anything from the...period?	عندكم أي شيء من العهد...؟ 'aandakum ay shay min al-'ahd...
Do I have to fill out any forms?	لازم أملأ أي استمارات؟ laazim amla' ay estimaaraat
Is there a certificate of authenticity?	هل هناك شهادة تثبت أنه أصلي؟ hal hunaak shahaada tusbit anahu aslee

Clothing

I'd like...	أريد... ooreed...
Can I try this on?	ممكن أجرب هذا؟ mumkin ujarrib haaza
It doesn't fit.	هذا ليس قياسي. haaza laysa qeeyaasee
It's too...	هو...جداً. huwa...jiddan
– big/small	كبير/صغير kabeer/sagheer
– short/long	قصير/طويل qaseer/taweel
– tight/loose	ضيق/واسع dayyik/waasia'
Do you have this in size...?	عندكم قياس...من هذا؟ 'aandakum qeeyaas...min fadlak
Do you have this in a *bigger/smaller* size?	عندكم قياس أكبر/أصغر من هذا؟ 'aandakum qeeyaas akbar/asghar min haaza

▶ For numbers, see page 168.

هذا يبدو رائعاً عليك. <u>haaza yab</u>doo <u>raa</u>'iaa a<u>lay</u>ik	That looks great on you.
هل القياس مناسب؟ hal al-qee<u>yaas</u> mu<u>naa</u>sib	How does it fit?
ليس عندنا قياسك. <u>lay</u>sa 'aandana qee<u>yaa</u>sak	We don't have your size.

You May See...

رجالي ri<u>jaa</u>lee	men's
نسائي ni<u>saa</u>'ee	women's
ولادي wa<u>laa</u>dee	children's

Color

I'd like something...	...أريد شيء oo<u>reed</u> shay...
– beige	بيج bayj
– black	أسود <u>as</u>wad
– blue	أزرق <u>az</u>raq
– brown	بني <u>bun</u>nee
– green	أخضر <u>akh</u>dar
– gray	رمادي ra<u>maa</u>dee
– orange	برتقالي burtu<u>qaa</u>lee
– pink	زهري <u>zah</u>ree
– purple	بنفسجي ba<u>naf</u>sajee
– red	أحمر <u>aH</u>mar
– white	أبيض <u>ab</u>yad
– yellow	أصفر <u>as</u>far

Clothes and Accessories

backpack	حقيبة ظهر Haqeebat zuhr
belt	حزام Hezaam
blouse	بلوزة blooza
bra	حمالة صدر Hamaalat sadr
briefs [underpants]	سروال داخلي sirwaal daakhilee
coat	معطف mi'ataf
dress	فستان fustaan
hat	قبعة qob'aa
headscarf	إيشارب eshaarib
jacket	جاكيت jaakeet
jeans	بنطلون جينز bantaloon jeenz
pajamas	بيجامة beejaama
pants [trousers]	بنطلون bantaloon
pantyhose [tights]	كولون kooloon
purse [handbag]	حقيبة يد Haqeebat yad
raincoat	معطف للمطر mi'ataf lil-matar
robe	جلابية jalaabeeya
scarf	لفاح lifaaH
shirt	قميص qamees
shorts	شورت shoort
skirt	تنورة tanoora
socks	جرابات juraabaat
suit	طقم taqm
sunglasses	نظارة شمسية nazaara shamseeya
sweater	كنزة صوف kanzat soof
sweatshirt	كنزة رياضة kanzat reeyaada

swimsuit	مايوه <u>maa</u>yoh
T-shirt	تي شيرت tee sheert
tie	كرافيت kra<u>veet</u>
underwear	ملابس داخلية ma<u>laa</u>bis dakhi<u>lee</u>ya

Fabric

I'd like...	أريد... oo<u>reed</u>...
– cotton	قطن qutn
– denim	جينز jeenz
– lace	تخريم takh<u>reem</u>
– leather	جلد jild
– linen	كتان ka<u>taan</u>
– silk	حرير Ha<u>reer</u>
– wool	صوف soof
Is it machine washable?	هل يمكن غسله في الغسالة؟ hal <u>yum</u>kin <u>gha</u>salhu feel gha<u>saa</u>la

---

i

The markets سوق (sooq) are a good place to buy traditional items such as robes and headscarves. Many countries also have a good range of locally made western-style clothes. Alternatively, you could buy the material and have your clothes made-to-measure by one of the many tailors you'll find in the Arabic world.

Shoes

I'd like...	أريد... oo<u>reed</u>...
– high-heels/flats	كعب عالي/زحف <u>ka</u>'ab <u>'aa</u>lee/zaHf
– boots	جزمة <u>jaz</u>ma
– loafers	موكاسان mookaa<u>saan</u>
– sandals	صندل <u>san</u>dal

– shoes	حذاء Hi<u>zaa</u>'
– slippers	شبشب <u>shib</u>shib
– sneakers	حذاء رياضة Hi<u>zaa</u>' ree<u>yaada</u>
In size...	نمرة... <u>num</u>ra...

▶ For numbers, see page 168.

Sizes

small (S)	صغير sa<u>ghee</u>r
medium (M)	متوسط muta<u>wass</u>it
large (L)	كبير ka<u>bee</u>r
extra large (XL)	كبير جداً ka<u>bee</u>r <u>jidd</u>an
petite	صغير جداً sa<u>ghee</u>r <u>jidd</u>an
plus size	قياسات أكبر qiyaa<u>saat</u> <u>ak</u>bar

Newsstand and Tobacconist

Do you sell English-language newspapers?	عندكم جرائد بالإنكليزي؟ '<u>aan</u>dakum ja<u>raa</u>'id bil-en<u>glee</u>zee
I'd like...	أريد... oo<u>ree</u>d...
– candy [sweets]	سكاكر sa<u>kaa</u>kir
– chewing gum	علكة '<u>il</u>ka
– a chocolate bar	لوح شوكلاتة looH shookoo<u>laa</u>ta
– a cigar	سيجار see<u>ghaa</u>r
– a *pack/carton* of cigarettes	باكيت/كروز سجائر *baa<u>keet</u>/krooz* si<u>jaa</u>'ir
– a lighter	ولاعة wa<u>laa</u>'a
– a magazine	مجلة ma<u>jalla</u>
– matches	كبريت kib<u>reet</u>
– a newspaper	جريدة ja<u>ree</u>da

I'd like…	ooreed… أريد....
– a postcard	kart boostaal كرت بوستال
– a road/town map of…	khareetat خريطة طرق/مدينة... toroq/madeenat…
– stamps	tawaabi'a طوابع

---

i Larger newsstands usually carry English-language newspapers and magazines, although they may be expensive and a few days old. You may be able to find local English-language papers, which will give you news and details about local events.

Photography

I'd like a/an… camera.	ooreed kaameera… أريد كاميرا...
– automatic	ootoomaateekeeya أوتوماتيكية
– digital	dijeetaal دجيتال
– disposable	lil-esti'amaal للاستعمال مرة واحدة marra waaHida
I'd like…	ooreed… أريد...
– a battery	bataareeya بطارية
– digital prints	suwwar dijeetaal صور دجيتال
– a memory card	kart zaakira كرت ذاكرة
Can I print digital photos here?	ممكن أطبع صور دجيتال هنا؟ mumkin atba' suwwar dijeetaal huna

Sports and Leisure

Essential

When's the *game/match*?	متى اللعبة؟ <u>mata</u> al-<u>lu</u>'aba
Where's…?	أين…؟ ayn…
– the beach	الشاطئ al-<u>shaa</u>tee'
– the park	الحديقة العامة al-Ha<u>dee</u>qat al-'<u>aa</u>ma
– the pool	المسبح al-<u>mas</u>baH
Is it safe to swim here?	هل هذا آمن للسباحة؟ hal <u>haza</u> <u>aa</u>min lil-si<u>baa</u>Ha
Can I rent [hire] golf clubs?	ممكن أستأجر مضارب غولف؟ <u>mum</u>kin as<u>ta</u>'ajir ma<u>daa</u>rib golf
How much per hour?	كم في الساعة؟ kam feel-<u>saa</u>'aa
How far is it to…?	كم بعيد…؟ kam ba<u>'eed</u>…
Show me on the map, please.	ممكن تريني على الخريطة؟ <u>mum</u>kin tu<u>ree</u>nee '<u>alal</u>-kha<u>ree</u>ta

Spectator Sports

When's…*game/match*?	متى لعبة…؟ <u>mata</u> <u>lu</u>'abat…
– the basketball	كرة السلة <u>kur</u>rat al-<u>silla</u>
– the boxing	الملاكمة al-mu<u>laa</u>kama
– the camel racing	سباق الجمال si<u>baaq</u> al-ja<u>maal</u>
– the falconry	الصيد بالصقور al-sayd bil-su<u>qoor</u>
– the golf	الغولف al-golf
– the horse racing	سباق الخيل si<u>baaq</u> al khayl

When's...*game/match*?	متى لعبة...؟ <u>ma</u>ta <u>lu</u>'abat...
– the soccer [football]	كرة القدم <u>ku</u>rrat al-<u>qa</u>dam
– the tennis	التنس al-tennis
– the volleyball	كرة الطائرة <u>ku</u>rrat al-<u>taa</u>'ira
Who's playing?	من يلعب؟ man <u>ya</u>l'ab
Where's the *racetrack/ stadium*?	أين مضمار السباق/الملعب؟ ayn mi<u>dmaar</u> al-si<u>baaq</u>/al-<u>mal</u>'ab

▶ For ticketing, see page 19.

i The Arab world is passionate about soccer. Going to watch a local game can be an experience and is something you can enjoy as a tourist without knowing the language. Games are usually held on Fridays.

Basketball, volleyball, squash and horseback riding are also popular. Some countries, such as the United Arab Emirates, offer a large variety of land- and water-based sports as well as local specialties such as camel racing and falconry. Many of these you can take part in as well as being a spectator.

Arab horses are famous the world over, and the desert is the ideal place to ride as long as you avoid the hottest part of the day. You will find stables all over the Middle East where you can rent horses by the hour or day.

Gambling is regarded as a sin in Islam.

Participating

Where *is/are*...?	أين...؟ ayn...
– the golf course	أرض الغولف ard al-golf
– the gym	النادي الرياضي al-<u>naa</u>dee al-ree<u>yaa</u>dee
– the park	الحديقة العامة al-Ha<u>dee</u>qat al-'aama
– the tennis courts	ملاعب التنس malaa'ib al-tennis

How much per...?	؟...كم الحساب في kam al-Hisaab fee...
– day	اليوم al-yohm
– hour	الساعة al-saa'aa
– game	اللعبة al-lu'aba
– round	الجولة al-johla
Can I rent [hire]...?	؟...ممكن أستأجر mumkin asta'ajir...
– clubs	مضارب غولف madaarib golf
– equipment	معدات mu'idaat
– a racket	مضرب midrab

At the Beach/Pool

Where's the *beach/ pool*?	أين الشاطئ/المسبح؟ ayn al-shaatee'/ al-masbaH
Is there...?	؟...هل هناك hal hunaak...
– a kiddie [paddling] pool	مسبح للأطفال masbaH lil-atfaal
– an *indoor/outdoor* pool	مسبح مسقوف/مكشوف masbaH masqoof/makshoof
– a lifeguard	منقذ munqiz

133

Is it safe...?	هل هذا آمن لـ...؟ hal haza aamin li...
– to swim	السباحة al-sibaaHa
– to dive	الغطس al-ghats
– for children	الأطفال al-atfaal

▶ For travel with children, see page 144.

I'd like to rent [hire]...	أريد أن أستأجر... ooreed an asta'ajir...
– a deck chair	كرسي للشاطئ kursee lil-shaatee'
– diving equipment	معدات الغوص mu'idaat lil-shaatee'
– a jet ski	جت سكي jet-ski
– a motorboat	زورق zohraq
– a rowboat	قارب للتجذيف qaarib lil-tajzeef
– snorkeling equipment	شنركل shnurkel
– a surfboard	لوح لركوب الأمواج looH li-rukoob al-amwaaj
– a towel	منشفة minshafa
– an umbrella	مظلة mazalla
– water skis	ألواح للتزحلق على الماء alwaaH lil-tazaHluq 'alal-maa'
– a windsurfer	لوح شراعي looH shiraa'ee
For...hours.	لمدة...ساعات. li-muddat...saa'aat.

▶ For travel with children, see page 144.

i

Some resort beaches are supervised, but many are not and you should take care to assess conditions before entering, particularly where children are concerned.
In coral reef areas (the Red Sea, for example), wear plastic shoes to protect your feet when swimming and be careful not to break off any of the coral, which is protected by law.

In the Countryside

Can I have a map of…, please?	ممكن خريطة لـ…من فضلك؟ mumkin khareeta li-…. min fadlak
– this region	هذه المنطقة hazih al-mantaqa
– the walking routes	طرق السير turuq al-sayr
– the bike routes	طرق الدراجات turuq al-darajaat
– the trails	الممرات al-mamaraat
Is it…?	هل هو…؟ hal huwa…
– easy	سهل sahil
– difficult	صعب su'ub
– far	بعيد ba'eed
– steep	شديد الانحدار shadeed al-enHedaar
How far is it to…?	كم بعيد…؟ kam ba'eed…
Show me on the map, please.	ممكن تريني على الخريطة، من فضلك؟ mumkin tureenee 'alal-khareeta min fadlak
I'm lost.	أنا تهت. ana tuhtu
Where's…?	أين…؟ ayn…
– the bridge	الجسر al-jisr
– the cave	الكهف al-kahf
– the cliff	المنحدر al-munHadar
– the desert	الصحراء al-saHraa'
– the farm	المزرعة al-mazra'aa
– the field	الحقل al-Haql
– the forest	الغابة al-ghaaba
– the hill	التل al-till
– the lake	البحيرة al-buHayra
– the mountain	الجبل al-jabal

135

Where's...?	أين...؟ ayn...
– the nature preserve	المحمية الطبيعية al-maHmeeya al-tabee'eeya
– the overlook [viewpoint]	الإطلالة al-etlaala
– the park	الحديقة العامة al-Hadeeqat al-'aama
– the path	الممر al-mamar
– the peak	القمة al-qimma
– the picnic area	منطقة النزهات mantaqat al-nuz-haat
– the pond	البركة al-baraka
– the river	النهر al-nahar
– the sea	البحر al-baHr
– the stream	الجدول al-jadwal
– the valley	الوادي al-waadee
– the waterfall	الشلال al-shalaal

Culture and Nightlife

Essential

What's there to do at night?	ماذا يمكننا أن نفعل في المساء؟ maaza yumkinena an naf'al feel masaa'
Do you have a program of events?	عندك برنامج الأنشطة؟ 'aandak barnaamij al-anshita
What's playing tonight?	ماذا يُعرَض الليلة؟ maaza yu'aarad al-layla
Where's...?	أين...؟ ayn...
– the downtown area	مركز المدينة markaz al-madeena
– the bar	البار al-baar
– the dance club	النادي الليلي al-naadee al-laylee
Is there a cover charge?	هل هناك رسم للخدمة؟ hal hunaak rasm lil-khidma

Bars and dance clubs can be found in Syria, Lebanon, Tunisia and Morocco. In other countries, these are mainly found in international hotels only.

There are casinos in Lebanon, and to a lesser extent, Syria.

A typical night out might include having dinner in a restaurant, which would generally have a singer and possibly a belly dancer. The restaurant might also have a dance floor for دبكة (dabke), a traditional folk dance from the Levant area where people hold hands and dance in a circle.

Entertainment

Can you recommend…?	ممكن تنصحني بـ...؟ <u>mum</u>kin tansa<u>H</u>nee bi…
– a concert	حفلة موسيقية <u>Haf</u>la mooseeqeeya
– a movie	فيلم feelm
– an opera	عرض أوبرا 'aard <u>oo</u>bira
– a play	مسرحية masra<u>Hee</u>ya
When does it *start/end*?	متى يبدأ/ينتهي؟ mata <u>yabda</u>'/ yan<u>ta</u>hee
Where's…?	أين...؟ ayn…
– the concert hall	قاعة الحفلات الموسيقية <u>qaa</u>'at al-Haf<u>laat</u> al-mooseeqeeya
– the opera house	دار الأوبرا daar al-<u>oo</u>bira
– the theater	المسرح al-<u>mas</u>raH
What's the dress code?	لازم نرتدي لباس معين؟ <u>laa</u>zim nar<u>ta</u>dee li<u>baas</u> mu'<u>aa</u>yan

137

I like…	أنا أحب... ana ooHibb…
– classical music	الموسيقى الكلاسيكية al-mooseeqa al-klaaseekeeya
– folk music	الموسيقى الشعبية al-mooseeqa al-sha'abeeya
– jazz	موسيقى الجاز mooseeqa al-jaaz
– pop music	موسيقى البوب mooseeqa al-poop
– rap	موسيقى الراب mooseeqa al-raap

▶ For ticketing, see page 19.

You May Hear…

| أطفئوا هواتفكم النقالة من فضلكم. at'fa'oo hawaatifkum al-naqaala min fadlikum | **Turn off your cell [mobile] phones, please.** |

i At your hotel or the tourist information centers, you'll often find publications listing local attractions: you can also consult English-language newspapers or the internet. Television programs are mostly in Arabic, but news and foreign films are usually broadcast in English—and some countries have a separate English-language channel. Most major hotels have English-language cable and satellite TV.

Nightlife

What's there to do at night?	ماذا يمكننا أن نفعل في المساء؟ maaza yumkinena an naf'al feel masaa'
Can you recommend…?	ممكن تنصحني بـ...؟ mumkin tansaHnee bi…
– a bar	بار baar
– a casino	كازينو kazeenoo

– a dance club	نادي ليلي <u>naa</u>dee <u>lay</u>lee
– a jazz club	نادي لموسيقى الجاز <u>naa</u>dee li-moo<u>see</u>qa al-jaaz
– a club with Arabic music	نادي ليلي فيه موسيقى عربية <u>naa</u>dee <u>lay</u>lee feeh moo<u>see</u>qa 'aara<u>bee</u>ya
Is there live music?	هل هناك موسيقى حية؟ hal hu<u>naak</u> moo<u>see</u>qa <u>Ha</u>ya
How do I get there?	كيف أصل إلى هناك؟ kayf <u>a</u>sil <u>i</u>la hu<u>naak</u>
Is there a cover charge?	هل هناك رسم للخدمة؟ hal hu<u>naak</u> rasm lil-<u>khid</u>ma
Let's go dancing.	لنذهب إلى مكان للرقص. li-<u>naz</u>hab <u>i</u>la ma<u>kaan</u> lil-raqs

▼ Special Needs

Business Travel

Essential

I'm here on business.	أنا هنا للعمل. <u>ana</u> <u>hu</u>na lil-'<u>aa</u>mal
Here's my business card.	هذا كرتي. <u>haza</u> <u>kar</u>tee
Can I have your card?	ممكن آخذ كرتك؟ <u>mum</u>kin <u>aa</u>khuz <u>kar</u>tak
I have a meeting with…	عندي اجتماع مع... '<u>aan</u>dee ejti<u>maa</u>' ma'…
Where's the…?	أين...؟ ayn…
– business center	مركز الأعمال <u>mar</u>kaz al-a'aa<u>maal</u>
– convention hall	قاعة المؤتمرات <u>qaa</u>'at al-mu'atama<u>raat</u>
– meeting room	قاعة الاجتماعات <u>qaa</u>'at al-ejtimaa'<u>aat</u>

---

i In formal meetings, people greet each other with a handshake. However, some devout Muslim men and some (not all) veiled women may not shake the hand of a person of the opposite sex. They'll hold their hand to their chest and say أنا لا أسلم (<u>ana</u> laa u<u>sal</u>lim) 'I don't shake hands'.

Business Communication

I'm here for a *seminar/conference.*

أنا هنا لحضور ندوة/لحضور مؤتمر.
ana huna li-Hudoor nadwa/li-Hudoor mu'atamar

My name is…

اسمي… esmee…

May I introduce my colleague…

ممكن أعرّفك على زميلي… mumkin u'aarifak 'ala zameelee…

I have *a meeting/an appointment* with…

عندي اجتماع/موعد مع… 'aandee ejtimaa'/moh'id ma'…

I'm sorry I'm late.

آسف♂/آسفة♀ على التأخير.
aasif ♂ /aasifa ♀ 'alal-ta'akheer

I need an interpreter.

أحتاج إلى مترجم. aHtaaj ila mutarjim

You can reach me at the…Hotel.

تستطيع أن تجدني في فندق…
tastatee'a an tajidnee fee funduq…

I'm here until...	أنا هنا حتى... _ana huna Hata..._

▶For days, see page 171.

I need to...	أحتاج أن... _aHtaaj an..._
– make a call	أجري اتصال هاتفي _oojree ettisaal haatifee_
– make a photocopy	أصور نسخة _oosawir nuskha_
– send an e-mail	أرسل بريد الكتروني _oorsil bareed elektroonee_
– send a fax	أرسل فاكس _oorsil faaks_
– send a package (overnight)	أرسل طرد بريدي (بحيث يصل غداً) _oorsil tard bareedee (bi-Hays yasil ghadaɪ)_
It was a pleasure to meet you.	فرصة سعيدة. _fursa sa'eeda_

▶For internet and communications, see page 50.

You May Hear...

عندك موعد؟ _'aandak moh'id_	Do you have an appointment?
مع من؟ _ma' man_	With whom?
هو♂/هي♀ في اجتماع. _huwa♂/hiya♀ fee ejtimaa'_	He/She is in a meeting.
لحظة من فضلك. _laHza min fadlak_	One moment, please.
تفضل بالجلوس. _tafaddal bil-juloos_	Have a seat.
هل تحب أن تشرب أي شيء؟ _hal tuHibb an tashrab ay shay_	Would you like something to drink?
شكراً لقدومك. _shukran ll-qudoomak_	Thank you for coming.

Travel with Children

Essential

Is there a discount for kids?	هل هناك خصم للأطفال؟ hal hunaak khasm lil-atfaal
Can you recommend a babysitter?	ممكن تنصحني بمربية أطفال؟ mumkin tansaHnee bi-murabeeyat al-atfaal
Do you have a *child's seat/ highchair*?	عندكم كرسي خاص للأطفال/كرسي عال؟ 'aandakum kursee khaas lil-atfaal/ kursee 'aalin
Where can I change the baby?	أين أستطيع تغيير حفاض الطفل؟ ayn astatee'a taghyeer Hifaad al-tifl

Fun with Kids

Can you recommend something for kids?	ممكن تنصحني بشيء للأطفال؟ <u>mum</u>kin tan<u>sa</u>Hnee bi-shay lil-at<u>faal</u>
Where's…?	أين…؟ ayn…
– the amusement park	مدينة الملاهي ma<u>dee</u>nat al-ma<u>laa</u>hee
– the arcade	قاعة الألعاب <u>qaa</u>'at al-al<u>'aab</u>
– the kiddie [paddling] pool	مسبح الأطفال <u>mas</u>baH al-at<u>faal</u>
– the park	الحديقة العامة al-Ha<u>dee</u>qat al-'<u>aa</u>ma
– the playground	الملعب al-<u>mal</u>'ab
– the zoo	حديقة الحيوانات Ha<u>dee</u>qat al-Hayawa<u>naat</u>
Are kids allowed?	مسموح دخول الأطفال؟ mas<u>mooH</u> du<u>khool</u> al-at<u>faal</u>
Is it safe for kids?	هل هو آمن للأطفال؟ hal <u>hu</u>wa aamin lil-at<u>faal</u>
Is it suitable for… year olds?	هل هو مناسب للأطفال الذين عمرهم…سنوات؟ hal <u>hu</u>wa mu<u>naa</u>sib lil-at<u>faal</u> ala<u>zeen</u> 'umruhum…sana<u>waat</u>

▶For numbers, see page 168.

You May Hear...

ما أجمله! maa aj<u>mal</u>hu	How cute!
ما اسمه♂/اسمها♀؟ maa <u>is</u>muhu♂/<u>is</u>muha♀	What's his/her name?
ما عمره♂/عمرها♀؟ maa '<u>um</u>ruhu♂/ '<u>um</u>ruha♀	How old is he/she?

145

Basic Needs for Kids

Do you have…?   عندكم...؟ 'aandakum…

– a baby bottle   رضّاعة ridaa'aa

– baby food   طعام أطفال ta'aam atfaal

– baby wipes   محارم للطفل maHaarim lil-tifl

– a car seat   مقعد طفل للسيارة maq'ad tifl lil-sayaara

– a children's *menu/ portion*   قائمة طعام/وجبات أصغر للأطفال qaa'imat ta'aam/wajabaat asghar lil-atfaal

▶ For dining with kids, see page 65.

– a *child's seat/ highchair*   كرسي خاص للأطفال/كرسي عال kursee khaas lil-atfaal/kursee 'aalin

– a *crib/cot*   مهد/سرير أطفال muhd/sareer atfaal

– diapers [nappies]   حفاضات Hifaadaat

– formula [baby food]   طعام للرضع ta'aam lil-radaa'

– a *pacifier* [soother]   لهّاية lahaaya

– a playpen   مكان محاط بالشباك للعب makaan muHaat bil-shubaak lil-la'ab

– a stroller [pushchair]   عربة أطفال 'aarabat atfaal

Can I breastfeed the baby here?   ممكن أرضع الطفل هنا؟ mumkin arda' al-tifl huna

Where can I *breastfeed/ change* the baby?   أين أستطيع أن أرضع/أغير حفاض الطفل؟ ayn astatee'a an oorade'a/ooghayer Hifaadaat al-tifl

Babysitting

Can you recommend a babysitter?   ممكن تنصحني بمربية أطفال؟ mumkin tansaHnee bi-murabeeyat al-atfaal

What do you charge?   كم تطلب؟ kam tatlub

I'll be back by…   سأعود قبلـ... sa-aa'ood qabl…

I can be reached at... تستطيع أن تتصل بي على الرقم...
tastatee'a an tatasil bee 'ala raqm...

Health and Emergency

Can you recommend a pediatrician?	ممكن تنصحني بطبيب أطفال؟ <u>mum</u>kin tan<u>saH</u>nee bi-ta<u>beeb</u> at<u>faal</u>
My child is allergic to...	طفلي يتحسس من... <u>tif</u>lee yata<u>Ha</u>sas min...
My child is missing.	طفلي مفقود <u>tif</u>lee maf<u>good</u>
Have you seen a *boy/girl*?	هل رأيت صبي/بنت؟ hal ra'<u>ee</u>ta *sabee/bint*

▶ For food items, see page 84.
▶ For health, see page 153.
▶ For police, see page 150.

For the Disabled

Essential

Is there...?	هل هناك...؟ hal hu<u>naak</u>...
– access for the disabled	مدخل مناسب للمعاقين <u>mad</u>khal mu<u>naa</u>sib lil-mu'aa<u>qeen</u>
– a wheelchair ramp	منحدر لكرسي المقعدين mun<u>Ha</u>dir li-<u>kur</u>see al-muq'aa<u>deen</u>
– a handicapped-[disabled-] accessible toilet	تواليت خاص للمقعدين toowaa<u>leet</u> khaas lil-muq'aa<u>deen</u>
I need...	أحتاج... aH<u>taaj</u>...
– assistance	مساعدة musaa'ada
– an elevator [a lift]	مصعد mis'ad
– a ground-floor room	غرفة في الطابق الأرضي <u>ghur</u>fa feel <u>taa</u>biq al-<u>ar</u>dee

Getting Help

I'm...	...أنا ana...
– disabled	معاق♂/معاقة♀ mu'aaq♂/mu'aaqa♀
– visually impaired	نظري ضعيف nazaree da'eef
– hearing impaired/ deaf	سمعي ضعيف/أصم sam'ee da'eef/asam
– unable to walk far	غير قادر♂/غير قادرة♀ على المشي بعيداً ghayr qaadir♂/ghayr qaadira♀ 'alal-mashee ba'eedan
– use the stairs	استخدام الدرج estikhdaam al-daraj
Please speak louder.	من فضلك ارفع صوتك. min fadlak 'irfa' sohtak
Can I bring my wheelchair?	ممكن أحضر كرسي المقعدين لي؟ mumkin aHdoor kursee al-muq'aadeen lee
Are guide dogs permitted?	هل كلاب إرشاد العميان مسموحة؟ hal kilaab ershaad al-'umyaan masmooHa
Can you help me?	ممكن تساعدني؟ mumkin tusaa'idnee
Please *open/hold* the door.	من فضلك افتح/امسك الباب. min fadlak eftaH/emsik al-baab

▼ Resources

Emergencies

Essential

Help!	النجدة! al-najda
Go away!	إمشي! emshee
Stop, thief!	امسك حرامي! emsik Haraamee
Get a doctor!	اتصل بدكتور! ettasil bil-doktoor
Fire!	حريق! Hareeq
I'm lost.	أنا تهت. ana tuht
Can you help me?	ممكن تساعدني؟ mumkin tusaa'idnee

Police

Essential

Call the police!	اتصل بالشرطة! ettasil bil-shurta
Where's the police station?	أين مركز الشرطة؟ ayn markaz al-shurta
There was an *accident/attack*.	وقع حادث/اعتداء. waqa'aa *Haadis/e'atidaa'*
My child is missing.	طفلي مفقود. tiflee mafqood
I need...	أحتاج إلى... aHtaaj ila...
– an interpreter	مترجم mutarjim
– to contact my lawyer	الاتصال بمحامي الخاص al-ettisaal bi-muHaamee al-khaas

– to make a phone call	إجراء اتصال هاتفي ejraa' ettisaal haatifee
I'm innocent.	أنا بريء♂/بريئة♀. ana baree'♂/baree'a♀

You May Hear...

املأ هذه الاستمارة. emlaa' hazih al-estimaara	Fill out this form.
هويتك الشخصية من فضلك. haweeyatak al-shakhseeya min fadlak	Your identification, please.
متى/أين حصل الحادث؟ mata/ayn hasal al-Haadis	*When/Where* did it happen?
ما أوصافه/أوصافها؟ maa ohsaafihi/ohsaafiha	What does he/she look like?

i Contact your consulate, ask the concierge at your hotel or ask the tourist information office for telephone numbers of the local ambulance, emergency services and police. If you need to make an emergency call you can ask someone for النجدة (al-najda), the help telephone number.

151

Lost Property and Theft

I'd like to report...	أريد التبليغ عن... ooreed al-tableegh 'aan...
– a mugging	سلب salb
– a rape	اغتصاب eghtisaab
– a theft	سرقة sirqa
I was *mugged/robbed*.	لقد سُلبت/سُرقت. laqad sulibtu/suriqtu
I lost my...	فقدت... faqadtu...
My...was stolen.	سُرقت مني... suriqat minee...
– backpack	حقيبة ظهر Haqeebat Zahr
– bicycle	دراجة daraaja
– camera	كاميرا kaameera
– (rental [hire]) car	سيارة (مستأجرة) sayaara (musta'ajara)
– computer	كومبيوتر kambyootir
– credit card	بطاقة ائتمان bitaaqat al-e'atimaan
– jewelry	مجوهرات mujoharaat
– money	مال maal
– passport	جواز سفر jawaaz safar
– purse [handbag]	حقيبة يد Haqeebat yad
– traveler's checks [cheques]	شيكات سياحية sheekaat seeyaaHeeya
– wallet	محفظة miHfaza
I need a police report.	أحتاج إلى تقرير من الشرطة. aHtaaj ila taqreer min al-shurta

Health

Essential

I'm sick [ill].	أنا مريض♂/مريضة♀. ana mareed♂/ mareeda♀
I need an English-speaking doctor.	أحتاج طبيب يتكلم إنكليزي. aHtaaj tabeeb yatakallam engleezee
It hurts here.	يوجد ألم هنا. yujad 'alam huna
I have a stomachache.	معدتي تؤلمني. mi'adatee tu'alimnee

Finding a Doctor ———————

Can you recommend a *doctor/dentist*?	ممكن تنصحني بطبيب/بطبيب أسنان؟ mumkin tansaHnee bi-tabeeb/ bi-tabeeb asnaan
Can the doctor come here?	ممكن أن يأتي الطبيب إلى هنا؟ mumkin an ya'atee al-tabeeb ila huna
I need an English-speaking doctor.	أحتاج طبيب يتكلم إنكليزي. aHtaaj tabeeb yatakallam engleezeeya
What are the office hours?	ما هي مواعيد العيادة؟ maa hiya mawaa'eed al-'iyaada
I'd like an appointment for...	أريد موعد... ooreed moh'id...
– today	لليوم lil-yohm
– tomorrow	للغد lil-ghad
– as soon as possible	بأسرع ما يمكن bi asraa' maa yumkin
It's urgent.	إنها حالة مستعجلة. inahaa Haala musta'ajila

Symptoms

I'm…	أنا… ana
– bleeding	أنزف anzif
– constipated	مصاب♂/مصابة♀ بإمساك musaab♂/ musaaba♀ bi-emsaak
– dizzy	أشعر بدوار ash'ur bi-duwaar
– nauseous	أشعر بغثيان ash'ur bi-ghasayaan
– vomiting	أتقيأ ataqaya'
It hurts here.	يوجد ألم هنا. yujad 'alam huna
I have…	عندي… 'aandee…
– an allergic reaction	حساسية Hasaaseeya
– chest pain	ألم في الصدر 'alam feel sadr
– cramps	تشنج tashanuj
– diarrhea	إسهال es-haal
– an earache	ألم في الأذن 'alam feel uzn
– a fever	حرارة مرتفعة Haraara murtafi'a
– pain	ألم 'alam
– a rash	طفح جلدي tafH jildee
– a sprain	التواء في المفصل eltiwaa' feel mifsal
– some swelling	انتفاخ entifaakh
– a sore throat	ألم في الحلق 'alam feel Halq
– a stomach ache	ألم في المعدة 'alam feel mi'ada
– sunstroke	ضربة شمس darbat shams
I've been sick [ill] for…days.	أنا مريض منذ…أيام. ana mareed munzu…ayaam

▶ For numbers, see page 168.

154

Health Conditions

I'm...	...أنا <u>a</u>na
– anemic	مصاب♂/مصابة♀ بفقر الدم mu<u>saab</u> ♂/mu<u>saaba</u> ♀ bi-fuqr al-dam
– asthmatic	مريض♂/مريضة♀ بالربو ma<u>reed</u>♂/ ma<u>reeda</u> ♀ bil-<u>rabu</u>
– diabetic	مريض ♂/مريضة♀ بالسكري ma<u>reed</u> ♂/ma<u>reeda</u> ♀ bil su<u>karee</u>
I'm allergic to *antibiotics/ penicillin*.	أتحسس من الحيوية/البنسلين ata<u>Has</u>as min al-<u>Haya</u>weeya/ al-binisi<u>leen</u>

▶ For food items, see page 84.

I have...	...عندي <u>'aan</u>dee...
– arthritis	التهاب مفاصل elti<u>haab</u> ma<u>faas</u>il
– a heart condition	قصور في القلب qu<u>soor</u> feel qalb
– *high/low* blood pressure	ضغط الدم مرتفع/منخفض <u>dagh</u>ut al-dam mur<u>tafi</u>'a/mun<u>Hafaz</u>
I'm on...	...أنا آخذ ana <u>aakh</u>iz...

You May Hear...

مم تشكو؟ mi<u>maa tash</u>koo	What's wrong?
أين يؤلمك؟ ayn u'a<u>lim</u>uk	Where does it hurt?
هل يؤلمك هنا؟ hal u'a<u>lum</u>ak <u>huna</u>	Does it hurt here?
هل تأخذ أي دواء؟ hal <u>ta</u>'akhuz ay da<u>waa</u>'	Are you on medication?
هل تتحسس من أي شيء؟ hal tata<u>Has</u>as min ay shay	Are you allergic to anything?

افتح فمك. eftaH famak	Open your mouth.
تنفس بعمق. tanafas bi-'umq	Breathe deeply.
اسعل من فضلك. us'ul min fadlak	Cough please.
اذهب لرؤية أخصائي. ezhab li-roo'ya akhsaa'ee	See a specialist.
اذهب إلى المستشفى. ezhab ilal mustashfa	Go to the hospital.
إنه... inahu...	It's...
مكسور maksoor	– broken
معد mu'din	– contagious
ملتهب multahib	– infected
ملتوي multawee	– sprained
غير خطير ghayr khateer	– nothing serious

Treatment

Do I need a *prescription/ medicine*?	هل أحتاج إلى وصفة طبية/دواء؟ hal aHtaaj ila *wasfa tibeeya/dawaa'*
Can you prescribe a generic drug?	ممكن تصف لي دواء بدون علامة تجارية؟ mumkin tasif lee dawaa' bidooni 'aalaama tijaareeya
Where can I get it?	أين أحصل عليه؟ ayn aHsal alayhi
Is this over the counter?	ممكن أشتري هذا بدون وصفة طبية؟ mumkin ashtaree haza bidooni wasfa tibeeya

▶ For dosage instructions, see page 159.

Hospital

Notify my family, please.	أخبر عائلتي من فضلك. ukhbir 'aa'ilatee min fadlak

I'm in pain.	أشعر بألم. ash'ur bi-'alam
I need a *doctor/nurse*.	أحتاج إلى طبيب/ممرض. aHtaaj ila tabeeb/mumarid
When are visiting hours?	ما هي مواعيد الزيارة؟ maa hiya mawaa'eed al-ziyaara
I'm visiting…	أنا هنا لأزور… ana huna li-azoor…

Dentist

I have…	عندي… 'aandee…
– a broken tooth	سن مكسور sin maksoor
– a lost filling	حشوة مفقودة Hashwa mafqooda
– a toothache	ألم في الأسنان 'alam feel asnaan
Can you fix this denture?	ممكن تصلح طقم الأسنان هذا؟ mumkin tusalliH taqm al-asnaan haza

Gynecologist

I have *cramps/a vaginal infection*.	عندي تشنج/التهاب مهبلي. 'aandee tashanuj/eltihaab mahbalee
I missed my period.	لم تأتي العادة الشهرية. lam ta'aati al-'aada al-shahreeya
I'm on the Pill.	آخذ حبوب منع الحمل. aakhuz Huboob mana'a al-Haml
I'm (…months) pregnant.	أنا حامل (في الشهر…). ana Haamil (feel shahr…)
I'm not pregnant.	أنا لست حامل. ana lastu Haamil
My last period was…	آخر عادة شهرية كانت… aakhar 'aada shahreeya kaanat…

Optician

I lost…	فقدت… faqadtu…
– a contact lens	عدسة لاصقة 'aadasa laasiqa
– my glasses	نظارتي nazaaratee
– a lens	عدسة 'aadasa

Payment and Insurance

How much?	كم الحساب؟ kam al-Hisaab
Can I pay by credit card?	ممكن أدفع ببطاقة الائتمان؟ mumkin 'adfa' bi-bitaaqat al-e'timaan
I have insurance.	عندي تأمين. 'aandee ta'ameen
I need a receipt for my insurance.	ممكن تعطيني إيصال لتأميني الصحي. mumkin tu'ateenee eesaal li-ta'ameenee al-siHee

Pharmacy [Chemist]

Where's the pharmacy [chemist]?	أين الصيدلية؟ ayn al-saydaleeya
What time does it *open/close*?	متى تفتح/تغلق؟ mata *taftaH/taghliq*
What would you recommend for…?	بم تنصحني لمعالجة…؟ bi-maa tansaHnee li-mu'aalaja
How much do I take?	كم جرعة؟ kam jur'aa
Can you fill [make up] this prescription?	ممكن تكتب لي وصفة طبية؟ mumkin taktub lee wasfa tibeeya
I'm allergic to…	أنا أتحسس من… ana ataHasas min…

 Pharmacies increasingly offer a wide range of imported toiletries and medicine, although the local alternatives will still be much cheaper. You may find you can obtain drugs over the counter that would be prescription-only back home, e.g., antibiotics or strong sedatives. The pharmacist will be able to advise you and even sometimes administer them. If in doubt, get a second opinion before deciding what to take. Pharmacies will usually post a notice that specifies which pharmacies are open late that particular week. Otherwise, hospitals can provide this information.

Dosage Instructions

How much do I take?	maa <u>hi</u>ya al-<u>jur</u>'aa ما هي الجرعة؟
How often?	kam <u>ma</u>ra كم مرة؟
Is it safe for children?	hal <u>huwa</u> munaasib lil-at<u>faal</u> هل هو مناسب للأطفال؟
I'm taking...	<u>ana</u> <u>aa</u>khuz... أنا آخذ...
Are there side effects?	hal hu<u>naak</u> aa<u>taar</u> jaani<u>bee</u>ya هل هناك آثار جانبية؟

You May See...

مرة/ثلاث مرات في اليوم _mara/talaat maraat_ feel yohm	*once/three times* a day
حبة _Habba_	tablet
قطرة _qatra_	drop
ملعقة صغيرة _mil'aaqa sagheera_	teaspoon
بعد/قبل/مع الوجبات _ba'ad/qabl/ma' al-wajabaat_	*after/before/with* meals
على معدة فارغة _'ala mi'ada faarigha_	on an empty stomach
ابتلعه كاملاً _ebtala'ahu kaamilan_	swallow whole
قد يسبب خمول _qad yusabib khumool_	may cause drowsiness
للاستعمال الخارجي فقط _lil-esti'amaal al-khaarijee faqat_	for external use only
سم _sam_	poison

Health Problems

I need something for...	أريد دواء لـ... _ooreed dawaa' li..._
– a cold	الرشح _al-rashH_
– a cough	السعال _al-su'aal_
– diarrhea	الإسهال _al-es-haal_
– insect bites	لدغات الحشرات _ladghaat al-Hasharaat_
– motion [travel] sickness	دوار السفر _dawaar al-safar_
– a sore throat	ألم الحلق _'alam al-Halq_
– sunburn	الحروق الشمسية _al-Hurooq al-shamseeya_
– an upset stomach	عسر الهضم _asr al-hadam_

Basic Needs

I'd like... | أريد ...ooreed

- acetaminophen [paracetamol] | سيتامول sitamol

- aftershave | عطر بعد الحلاقة utr ba'ad al-Halaaqa

- aspirin | أسبرين asbireen

- bandages | ضمادات damaadaat

- a comb | مشط misht

- condoms | واقيات ذكرية waaqiyaat zakareeya

- contact lens solution | محلول للعدسات اللاصقة maHlool lil-adasaat al-laasiqa

- deodorant | مزيل الرائحة muzeel al raa'il la

- a hairbrush | فرشاة الشعر furshaat al-sha'aar

- ibuprofen | إيبوبروفين ibuprofen

- insect repellent | مادة طاردة للحشرات maada taarida lil-Hasharaat

- lotion | غسول ghasool

- a (disposable) razor | موس الحلاقة (للاستعمال مرة واحدة) moos al-Hilaaqa (lil-esti'amaal mara waaHeda)

- razor blades | شفرات الحلاقة shafaraat al-Hilaaqa

- sanitary napkins [pads] | فوط نسائية fuwat nisaa'eeya

- shampoo/conditioner | شامبو/بلسم shampoo/balsam

- soap | صابون saboon

- sunscreen | واقي الشمس waaqee al-shams

- tampons | سدادات قطنية للسيدات sadadaat qutneeya lil-sayidaat

- tissues | مناديل ورقية manaadeel warqeeya

- toilet paper | ورق تواليت warq toowaaleet

- toothpaste | معجون أسنان ma'aajoon asnaan

▶ For baby products, see page 146.

161

Reference

Grammar

Regular Verbs

Arabic verbs add prefixes and endings to a base form to make the different persons and tenses. This base form is shown as the third person singular of the present tense, which is the form given in the dictionary in this book, as corresponding to the English infinitive. Here is one example of one type of a regular Arabic verb.

TO WRITE	Present	Past	Future
I (انا) (ana)*	اكتب aktub	كتبتُ katabtu	ساكتب sa-aktub
you (♂ sing.) (انتَ) (anta)	تكتب taktub	كتبتَ katabta	ستكتب sa-taktub
you (♀ sing.) (انتِ) (anti)	تكتبين taktubeen	كتبتِ katabtee	ستكتبين sa-taktubeen
he (هو) (huwa)	يكتب yaktub	كتب katab	سيكتب sa-yaktub
she (هي) (hiya)	تكتب taktub	كتبت katabat	ستكتب sa-taktub
we (نحن) (naHna)	نكتب naktub	كتبنا katabna	سنكتب sa-naktub
you (pl.) (انتم) (antum)	تكتبون taktuboon	كتبتم katabtum	ستكتبون sa-taktuboon
they (هم) (hum)	يكتبون yaktuboon	كتبوا kataboo	سيكتبون sa-yaktuboon

Irregular Verbs

Irregular verbs in Arabic must be memorized. Two commonly used irregular verbs, "to be" and "to sell", are conjugated below.

"To be" is an unusual verb, since it has no present tense. For example, "He is a doctor" would be هو طبيب huwa tabeeb (he doctor) or "she is sick" هي مريضة hiya mareeda (she sick).

---

*Arabic pronouns are often omitted in speech, unless special emphasis is required.

TO BE	Past	Future
I (أنا) (<u>a</u>na)	كنتُ <u>kun</u>tu	ساكون sa-a<u>koon</u>
you (♂ sing.) (أنتَ) (<u>an</u>ta)	كنتَ <u>kun</u>ta	ستكون sa-ta<u>koon</u>
you (♀ sing.) (أنتِ) (<u>an</u>ti)	كنتِ <u>kun</u>tee	ستكونين sa-ta<u>koon</u>een
he (هو) <u>hu</u>wa	كان kaan	سيكون sa-ya<u>koon</u>
she (هي) (<u>hi</u>ya)	كانت <u>kaa</u>nat	ستكون sa-ta<u>koon</u>
we (نحن) (<u>naH</u>na)	كنا <u>kun</u>na	سنكون sa-na<u>koon</u>
you (pl.) (أنتم) (<u>an</u>tum)	كنتم <u>kun</u>tum	ستكونون sa-ta<u>koon</u>oon
they (هم) (hum)	كانوا <u>kaa</u>noo	سيكونون sa-ya<u>koon</u>oon

TO SELL	Present	Past	Future
I (أنا) (<u>a</u>na)	أبيع a<u>bee</u>'a	بعتُ <u>bi</u>'tu	سابيع sa-a<u>bee</u>'a
you (♂ sing.) (أنتَ) (<u>an</u>ta)	تبيع ta<u>bee</u>'a	بعتَ <u>bi</u>'ta	ستبيع sa-ta<u>bee</u>'a
you (♀ sing.) (أنتِ) (<u>an</u>ti)	تبيعين ta<u>bee</u>'een	بعتِ <u>bi</u>'tee	ستبيعين sa-ta<u>bee</u>'een
he (هو) (<u>hu</u>wa)	يبيع ya<u>bee</u>'a	باع baa'a	سيبيع sa-ya<u>bee</u>'a
she (هي) (<u>hi</u>ya)	تبيع ta<u>bee</u>'a	باعت <u>baa</u>'at	ستبيع sa-ta<u>bee</u>'a
we (نحن) (<u>naH</u>na)	نبيع na<u>bee</u>'a	بعنا <u>bi</u>'na	سنبيع sa-na<u>bee</u>'a
you (pl.) sold (أنتم) (<u>an</u>tum)	تبيعون ta<u>bee</u>'oon	بعتم <u>bi</u>'tum	ستبيعون sa-ta<u>bee</u>'oon
they (هم) (hum)	يبيعون ya<u>bee</u>'oon	باعوا <u>baa</u>'oo	سيبيعون sa-ya<u>bee</u>'oon

Nouns

Nouns in Arabic are either masculine or feminine. Masculine nouns can end in any letter except "a": موظف mu<u>wazz</u>af (clerk, official), مسافر mu<u>saa</u>fir (passenger), رجل <u>ra</u>jul (man), بيت bayt (house). Feminine nouns usually end in "a": محطة ma<u>Ha</u>ta (station), سيارة sa<u>yaa</u>ra (car), رخصة <u>rukh</u>sa (license). There are a few common feminine words that do not end in "a", such as أم umm (mother), أخت ukht (sister), بنت bint (daughter, girl).

The regular plural for masculine nouns is formed by adding "een": موظفين muwazza<u>feen</u> (officials), مسافرين musaafi<u>reen</u> (passengers).

The regular plural for feminine nouns is formed by adding "aat": محطات maHat<u>aat</u> (stations), سيارات saya<u>raat</u> (cars).

Many nouns, mainly masculine, have irregular plurals. Typical are: رجال ri<u>jaal</u> (men), بيوت bu<u>yoot</u> (houses), بنات ba<u>naat</u> (girls), أمهات uma<u>haat</u> (mothers).

Dual Plurals

As well as singular and plural, Arabic also has a dual ending that is used when referring to two things as the objects of a verb.

For masculine nouns you add the ending "ayn": كتاب ki<u>taab</u> (a book), كتابين kitaa<u>bayn</u> (two books). For feminine nouns you add "tayn": تذكرة <u>taz</u>kara (a ticket), تذكرتين tazkara<u>tayn</u> (two tickets).

Articles

There is no equivalent to the indefinite articles "a" or "an" in Arabic.

The definite article (the) in Arabic is الـ "al-"; simply put "al-" before the noun: الرجل al-<u>ra</u>jul (the man), البنت al-bint (the girl); الرجال al-ri<u>jaal</u> (the men), البنات al-ba<u>naat</u> (the girls).

Word Order

In Arabic, word order is usually as in English: subject – verb – object.

Here are two Arabic phrases taken from this book, which we can compare with the English version:

أريد أن أستأجِر قارب للتجذيف.
oo<u>reed</u> an asta'ajir <u>qaa</u>rib lil-taj<u>zeef</u> I'd like to rent a rowboat.

I'd like (oo<u>reed</u>) to rent (an asta'ajir) a rowboat (<u>qaa</u>rib lil-taj<u>zeef</u>)

هل هناك أي تخفيضات؟
hal hu<u>naak</u> ay takhfeed<u>aat</u> Are there any discounts?

Are (hal/question word) there (hunaak) any (ay) discounts (takhfeed<u>aat</u>)?

Negation

The usual way of negating a verb is to put لا laa (not) in front of the present tense of the verb:

آخذها.
aa<u>kh</u>ud-haa I take it.

لا آخذها.
laa aa<u>kh</u>ud-haa I don't take it.

Imperatives

To form the imperative, take the second person present tense form (singular or plural) such as تكتب <u>tak</u>tub or تكتبون <u>tak</u>tu<u>boon</u> (you write), replace the "t" with "e" and then remove the final "n" in the plural):

اكتب!\اكتبوا!
<u>ek</u>tub/<u>ek</u>tuboo Write!

To give a negative command, just take the second person present tense form as it is, and add the prefix لا laa:

لا تكتب!
laa <u>tak</u>tub Don't write!

Comparative and Superlative

The comparative is formed by taking the adjective, adding an "a" at the beginning and replacing the other vowel with an "a". The superlative is formed adding ال al- to the comparative form:

كبير		أكبر		الأكبر
ka<u>beer</u> (big)	→	<u>ak</u>bar (bigger)	→	al-<u>ak</u>bar (the biggest)
صغير		أصغر		الأصغر
sa<u>gheer</u> (small)	→	<u>asghar</u> (smaller)	→	al-<u>asghar</u> (the smallest)

Personal Pronouns

The personal pronouns are as follows:

أنا	<u>a</u>na	I
أنتَ	<u>an</u>ta	you (♂ sing.)
أنتِ	<u>an</u>ti	you (♀ sing.)
هو	<u>hu</u>wa	he
هي	<u>hi</u>ya	she
نحن	<u>naH</u>na	we
أنتم	<u>an</u>tum	you (pl.)
هم	hum	they

Unlike most other languages, as can be seen from the verb tables on pages 162–163, the verb form changes depending whether you are addressing a man or a woman:

أنتَ تكتب.
<u>an</u>ta <u>tak</u>tub You (♂) are writing.

أنت تكتبين.
<u>an</u>ti taktu<u>been</u> You (♀) are writing.

In this book, for simplicity, we have as a general rule given Arabic translations that are used for talking to a man.

Possessive Pronouns

Possessive pronouns in Arabic are shown in the form of suffixes to the noun:

ـ(تَ)ـي	-(t)ee	my
ـ(تَ)ـك	-(t)ak	your (♂ sing.)
ـ(تَ)ـك	-(t)ek	your (♀ sing.)
ـه	-uh	his
ـها	-ha	her
ـنا	-na	our

كـم	-kum	your (pl.)
ـهم	-hum	their

These suffixes are never stressed.

كتاب		كتابي	
ki<u>taab</u> (a book)	→	ki<u>taa</u>bee (my book)	

غرفة		غرفتي	
<u>ghur</u>fa (a room)	→	<u>ghur</u>fatee (my room)	

فندق		فندقنا	
<u>fun</u>duq (a hotel)	→	<u>fun</u>duqna (our hotel)	

Adjectives

Adjectives agree with the gender of the nouns they describe. To form the feminine, add an -a to the masculine.

♂جديد	♀جديدة
ja<u>deed</u> (new)	ja<u>dee</u>da

♂بيت		بيت جديد
bayt (a house)	→	bayt ja<u>deed</u> (a new house)

and

♀سيارة		سيارة جديدة
sa<u>yaa</u>ra (a car)	→	sa<u>yaa</u>ra ja<u>dee</u>da (a new car)

For inanimate plurals, the feminine singular adjective is used:

♂بيوت		بيوت جديدة
bu<u>yoot</u> (houses)	→	bu<u>yoot</u> ja<u>dee</u>da (new houses)

and

♀سيارات		سيارات جديدة
sayaa<u>raat</u> (cars)	→	sayaa<u>raat</u> ja<u>dee</u>da (new cars)

Numbers

Essential

	Numeral	Word
0	٠	صفر sifr
1	١	واحد <u>waa</u>Hid
2	٢	اثنان et<u>naan</u>
3	٣	ثلاثة ta<u>laa</u>ta
4	٤	أربعة <u>'arb</u>a'a
5	٥	خمسة <u>kham</u>sa
6	٦	ستة <u>sit</u>ta
7	٧	سبعة <u>sab</u>'aa
8	٨	ثمانية ta<u>maa</u>niya
9	٩	تسعة <u>tis</u>'aa
10	١٠	عشرة <u>'aa</u>shara
11	١١	أحد عشر <u>a</u>Had <u>'aa</u>shar
12	١٢	اثنا عشر et<u>naa</u> <u>'aa</u>shar
13	١٣	ثلاثة عشر ta<u>laa</u>tat <u>'aa</u>shar
14	١٤	أربعة عشر <u>'arb</u>a'at <u>'aa</u>shar
15	١٥	خمسة عشر <u>kham</u>sat <u>'aa</u>shar
16	١٦	ستة عشر <u>sit</u>tat <u>'aa</u>shar
17	١٧	سبعة عشر <u>sab</u>'aat <u>'aa</u>shar
18	١٨	ثمانية عشر ta<u>maa</u>niyat <u>'aa</u>shar
19	١٩	تسعة عشر <u>tis</u>'aat <u>'aa</u>shar
20	٢٠	عشرون '<u>ash</u>ro<u>on</u>

21	٢١	واحد و عشرون <u>waa</u>Hid wa-'ash<u>roon</u>
22	٢٢	اثنان و عشرون et<u>naan</u> wa-'ash<u>roon</u>
30	٣٠	ثلاثون talaa<u>toon</u>
31	٣١	واحد و ثلاثون <u>waa</u>Hid wa-talaa<u>toon</u>
40	٤٠	أربعون 'arba<u>'oon</u>
50	٥٠	خمسون kham<u>soon</u>
60	٦٠	ستون sit<u>toon</u>
70	٧٠	سبعون sab<u>'oon</u>
80	٨٠	ثمانون tamaa<u>noon</u>
90	٩٠	تسعون tis<u>'oon</u>
100	١٠٠	مائة <u>mi</u>'a
101	١٠١	مائة و واحد <u>mi</u>'a wa-<u>waa</u>Hid
200	٢٠٠	مائتان mi'a<u>taan</u>
500	٥٠٠	خمسمائة khams<u>mi</u>'a
1,000	١٠٠٠	ألف alf
10,000	١٠٠٠٠	عشرة آلاف '<u>aa</u>sharat a<u>laaf</u>
1,000,000	١٠٠٠٠٠٠	مليون mil<u>yoon</u>

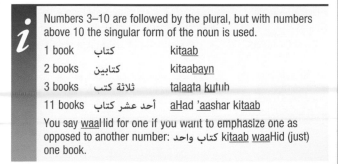

i

Numbers 3–10 are followed by the plural, but with numbers above 10 the singular form of the noun is used.

1 book	كتاب	ki<u>taab</u>
2 books	كتابين	kitaa<u>bayn</u>
3 books	ثلاثة كتب	ta<u>laa</u>ta <u>ku</u>tub
11 books	أحد عشر كتاب	a<u>Had</u> '<u>aa</u>shar ki<u>taab</u>

You say <u>waa</u>lid for one if you want to emphasize one as opposed to another number: كتاب واحد ki<u>taab</u> <u>waa</u>Hid (just) one book.

169

Ordinal Numbers

first	أول	<u>oh</u>wal
second	ثاني	<u>taa</u>nee
third	ثالث	<u>taa</u>lit
fourth	رابع	<u>raa</u>bi'a
fifth	خامس	<u>khaa</u>mis
once	مرّة	<u>marra</u>
twice	مرّتان	marra<u>taan</u>
three times	ثلاث مرّات	ta<u>laat</u> mar<u>raat</u>

Time

Essential

What time is it?	كم الساعة؟ kam al-<u>saa</u>'a
It's noon [midday].	الوقت منتصف النهار al-waqt mun<u>ta</u>sef al-na<u>haar</u>
At midnight.	في منتصف الليل fee mun<u>ta</u>sef al-layl
From one o'clock to two o'clock.	من الساعة الواحدة حتى الساعة الثانية. min al-<u>saa</u>'a al-<u>waa</u>Hida <u>H</u>atta al-<u>saa</u>'a al-<u>taa</u>niya
Five after [past] three.	الساعة الثالثة و خمس دقائق. al-<u>saa</u>'a al-<u>taa</u>lita wa-khams da<u>qaa</u>'iq
A quarter to four.	الساعة الرابعة إلا ربع. al-<u>saa</u>'a al-<u>raa</u>bi'a <u>ell</u>a rub'
5:30 a.m./p.m.	الساعة الخامسة و النصف صباحاً\مساءاً. al-<u>saa</u>'a al-<u>khaa</u>misa wa-nusf *sabaaHan/ masaa'an*

i The 24-hour clock is used only for the timing of TV programs. For all other purposes, you need to specify whether it is morning (4–11 a.m.) صباحا (sabaaHan), noon (12, 1) ظهرا (zuhran), afternoon (2–4 p.m.) بعد الظهر (ba'ad al-zuhur), evening (5–9 p.m.) مساء (masaa'an) or night (10 p.m.–3 a.m.) ليلا laylan.

Days

Monday	الاثنين	al-et<u>nayn</u>
Tuesday	الثلاثاء	al-tula<u>taa'</u>
Wednesday	الأربعاء	al-'arba<u>'aa</u>
Thursday	الخميس	al-kha<u>mees</u>
Friday	الجمعة	al-<u>jom</u>'a
Saturday	السبت	al-sabt
Sunday	الأحد	al-<u>aHd</u>

Dates

yesterday	البارحة	umbaariH
today	اليوم	al-yohm
tomorrow	غداً	ghadan
day	يوم	yohm
week	أسبوع	usboo'
month	شهر	shahr
year	سنة	sana

Months

	Most Arabic-speaking regions		Syria/the Levant	
January	يناير	yanaayir	كانون الثاني	kaanoon al-taanee
February	فبراير	fibraayir	شباط	shubaat
March	مارس	mars	آذار	azaar
April	ابريل	ebreel	نيسان	nisaan
May	مايو	maayo	أيار	ayaar
June	يونيو	yooniyoo	حزيران	Haziraan
July	يوليو	yooliyoo	تموز	tammooz
August	أغسطس	aghustus	آب	ab
September	سبتمبر	septembir	أيلول	aylool
October	أكتوبر	octobir	تشرين الأول	tishreen al-ohwal
November	نوفمبر	novembir	تشرين الثاني	tishreen al-taanee
December	ديسمبر	decembir	كانون الأول	kaanoon al-ohwal

172

i The Islamic lunar hijra calendar has 12 months, but is 10 to 11 days shorter than the Gregorian calendar. A.D. 2000 is A.H. 1419/1420 in the hijra calendar.

Seasons

in/during…	في\خلال	fee/khil<u>aal</u>
the spring	الربيع	al-ra<u>bee</u>'
the summer	الصيف	al-sayf
the fall [autumn]	الخريف	al-kha<u>reef</u>
the winter	الشتاء	al-shi<u>taa</u>'

Holidays

January 1: New Year's Day (celebrated everywhere except the Gulf)

Easter: (celebrated everywhere except the Gulf) Both the Orthodox and Catholic Easters are celebrated, with public holidays on both occasions for Easter Sunday (Good Friday, Easter Sunday and Easter Monday in Lebanon).

May 1: Labor Day

December 25: Christmas Day (celebrated everywhere except the Gulf) is celebrated by Christians and increasingly by non-Christians – but more as an occasion for children to enjoy Christmas trees and Santa Claus than as a religious occasion.

There are also country-specific national holidays such as Independence Day, Martyrs' Day, Anniversary of the Revolution, etc.

Four major Muslim holidays, which move in accordance with the lunar calendar are:

عيد الفطر 'ayd al-fitr: Feast of breaking the fast celebrates the end of Ramadan (the Muslim holy month). It lasts about three days, during which families visit friends and relatives, and give to charity.

عيد الأضحى 'ayd al-<u>az</u>Ha: Feast of the Sacrifice comes 70 days after Ramadan and lasts four days. Many Muslim families slaughter a sheep and share the meat with relatives or donate to the poor.

رأس السنة الهجرية ras al-<u>sa</u>na al-hij<u>ree</u>ya: Islamic New Year

عيد المولد النبوي 'ayd al-<u>moh</u>lid al-<u>nab</u>awee: The Prophet's Birthday (Muhammad)

The month of Ramadan رمضان (rama<u>daan</u>) is the Muslim month of fasting and lasts for approximately 28 days. As the Muslim calendar is a lunar one, the date for Ramadan moves year to year. An internet search for Ramadan or your travel agent should be able to tell you the likely dates for a specific year.

During Ramadan many Muslims refrain from eating, drinking or smoking between sunrise and sunset as a communal display of religious faith. Eating habits and meal times change accordingly. The main meals of the day are سحور (su<u>Hoor</u>), a pre-dawn snack, and إفطار (if<u>taar</u>), the sunset main meal that breaks the fast. There are specific drinks and dishes consumed during Ramadan. One of the most famous drinks is قمر الدين (<u>qa</u>mar al-deen), a type of thick juice made from dried apricot paste. You will find that many international hotels offer both إفطار (if<u>taar</u>) at sunset and then dinner later during Ramadan.

Generally cities come to life at night during Ramadan and people go out until the early hours of the morning. Shops are also often open very late.

If you are visiting a Muslim country during Ramadan you will usually be able to find places to eat during the day that cater to tourists or non-Muslims. Out of courtesy, however, you should try to avoid eating or smoking in public places during daylight hours.

Conversion Tables

When you know	Multiply by	To find
ounces	28.3	grams
pounds	0.45	kilograms
inches	2.54	centimeters
feet	0.3	meters
miles	1.61	kilometers
square inches	6.45	sq. centimeters
square feet	0.09	sq. meters
square miles	2.59	sq. kilometers
pints (U.S./Brit)	0.47/0.56	liters
gallons (U.S./Brit)	3.8/4.5	liters
Fahrenheit	5/9, after −32	Centigrade
Centigrade	9/5, then +32	Fahrenheit

Mileage

1 km – 0.62 mi	20 km – 12.4 mi
5 km – 3.1 mi	50 km – 31 mi
10 km – 6.2 mi	100 km – 61 mi

Measurement

1 gram	واحد غرام waaHid gram	= 0.035 oz.
1 kilogram (kg)	واحد كيلوغرام waaHid kilogram	= 2.2 lb
1 liter (l)	واحد ليتر waaHid leetir	= 1.06 U.S/0.88 Brit. quarts
1 centimeter (cm)	واحد سنتمتر waaHid santimeter	– 0.4 inch
1 meter (m)	واحد متر waaHid meter	= 3.28 ft.
1 kilometer (km)	واحد كيلومتر waaHid kilometer	= 0.62 mile

Temperature

-40° C – -40° F	-1° C – 30° F	20° C – 68° F
-30° C – -22° F	0° C – 32° F	25° C – 77° F
-20° C – -4° F	5° C – 41° F	30° C – 86° F
-10° C – 14° F	10° C – 50° F	35° C – 95° F
-5° C – 23° F	15° C – 59° F	

Oven Temperature

100° C – 212° F	177° C – 350° F
121° C – 250° F	204° C – 400° F
149° C – 300° F	260° C – 500° F

Related Websites

www.tsa.gov (U.S.)
www.caa.co.uk (U.K.)
for airport safety information

www.travel.state.gov (U.S.)
www.fco.gov.uk (U.K.)
for consulate or embassy information

www.towd.com
www.antor.com
for tourist information offices by country

www.hihostels.com
for hostel reservations and information

www.berlitzpublishing.com
www.insightguides.com
for travel guides

www.geocities.com/bruastronomy/ sunmoon_hijrah_calculator.htm
for date conversions

English–Arabic Dictionary

A

accept يقبل yaqbal

access مدخل madkhal

access v (internet) يدخل yadkhul

accident حادث Haadis

accompany يرافق yuraafiq

account حساب Hisaab

acetaminophen سيتامول sitamol

acupuncture علاج بالإبر elaaj bil ibar

adapter محوّل muHawwil

address عنوان unwaan

admission (to museum etc) رسم الدخول rasm al-dukhool

after بعد ba'ad

afternoon بعد الظهر ba'ad al-zuhr

aftershave عطر بعد الحلاقة utr ba'ad al-Halaaqa

age عمر umr

agency وكالة wakaala

AIDS أيدز AIDS

air conditioner مكيف الهواء mukayyef al-hawaa

airline خطوط جوية khutoot johweeya

airplane طائرة taa'ira

airport مطار mataar

air pump منفاخ minfakh

aisle seat مقعد على الممشى maq'ad 'alal mamsha

Algeria الجزائر al-jazaa'ir

Algerian جزائري jazaa'iree

allergic يعاني من الحساسية yu'aanee min al-Hasaaseeya

allowed مسموح masmooH

alone بمفرده bi-munfaridih

alter يعدل yu'addel

alternate route طريق آخر tareeq aakhar

aluminum foil رقائق المنيوم raqaa'iq aluminyoom

amazing مدهش mud-hish

ambulance سيارة الإسعاف sayaarat al-es'aaf

American adj أمريكي amreekaanee

amusement park مدينة الملاهي madeenat al-malaahee

anemic مصاب بفقر الدم musaab bi-fuqr al-dam

anesthesia تخدير takhdeer

animal حيوان Haywaan

ankle كاحل kaaHil

another آخر aakhar

antibiotics المضادات الحيوية mudadaat al-Hayaweeya

antiques store محل الأنتيكات maHal al-antikaat

antiseptic cream كريم معقم kreem mu'aaqim

anything أي شيء ay shay

apartment شقة shiqqa

appendix الزائدة الدودية zaa'ida al-doodeeya

appointment موعد moh'id

Arab (person) عربي aarabee

adj	adjective	BE	British English	v	verb
adv	adverb	n	noun

Arabic *adj* عربي 'aarabee; *n*
(language) العربية al-'aarabeeya
arcade قاعة الألعاب qaa'at al-al'aab
area code رمز المنطقة ramz
al-mantaqa
arm ذراع ziraa'
aromatherapy علاج أروماتي 'elaaj
aroomaatee
arrivals (airport) الوصول qudoom
arrive يصل yasil
arthritis التهاب مفاصل eltihaab
mafaasil
aspirin أسبرين asbireen
assistance مساعدة musaa'ada
asthmatic مريض بالربو mareed bil-rabu
ATM الصراف الآلي saraaf al-aalee
attack (on person) اعتداء e'atidaa'
attraction (sightseeing) المعلم
الرئيسية ma'aalim al-ra'eeseeya
attractive (person) جذاب jazaab
Australia أستراليا ostraaleeya
Australian أسترالي ostraalee
automatic أوتوماتيكي
ootoomaateekee
available غير مشغول ghayr
mashghool

B

baby رضيع radee'a
baby bottle رضّاعة ridaa'aa
baby food طعام للرضع ta'aam
lil-rada'
babysitter مربية أطفال murabeeyat
atfaal
baby wipe محارم للطفل maHaarim
lil-tifl
back (of body) ظهر zuhr
backache ألم في الظهر 'alam feel zuhr

backpack حقيبة ظهر Haqeebat zuhr
bad رديء radee'
bag كيس kees
baggage claim استلام الحقائب
estelaam al-Haqaa'ib
Bahrain البحرين baHrayn
Bahraini بحريني baHraynee
bakery المخبز makhbaz
ballet عرض باليه 'aard baalay
bandage ضمادات damaad
bank بنك bank
bar بار baar
barber حلاق رجالي Halaaq rijaalee
baseball البايسبول "baseball"
basket سلة silla
basketball كرة السلة kurrat al-silla
bathroom حمام Hamaam
battery بطارية bataareeya
be يكون yakoon
beach شاطىء shaatee'
beautiful جميل jameel
bed سرير sareer
before قبل qabl
begin يبدأ yabda'
beginner مبتدىء mubtadi'
behind خلف khalf
beige بيج bayj
belt حزام Hezaam
best الأحسن al-aHsan
bet *n* مراهنة muraahana
better أفضل afdal
bicycle دراجة daraaja
big كبير kabeer
bikini wax شمع خط البيكيني shama'
khat al-beekeenee
bill *n* حساب Hisaab
bird طير tayr
birthday عيد ميلاد 'aayd meelaad
black أسود aswad

bladder مثانة masaana
blanket بطانية bataneeya
bleed ينزف yanzif
blender خلاط khalaat
blood دم dam
blood pressure ضغط الدم dught al-dam
blouse بلوزة blooza
blue أزرق azraq
boarding pass بطاقة صعود bitaaqat su'ood
boat قارب qaarib
boat trip رحلة بالقارب riHla bil-qaarib
bone عظم 'azm
book كتاب kitaab
bookstore مكتبة maklaba
boot جزمة jazma
boring ممل mumill
botanical garden حديقة النباتات Hadeeqat al-nabataat
bottle زجاجة zujaaja
bottle opener فتاحة زجاجات fataaHat zujajaat
bowl زبدية zubdeeya
box علبة 'ulba
boxing ملاكمة mulaakama
boy صبي sabee
boyfriend صاحب saaHib
bra حمالة صدر Hamaalat sadr
bracelet سوار siwaar
brake فرامل faraamil
break (tooth, bone) يكسر yukassir
breakdown تعطل ta'aatul
breakfast فطور futoor
break-in اقتحام oqtil laam
breast ثدي saddee
breastfeed ترضّع turaddi
breath يتنفس yatanaffas
bridge جسر jisr

briefs سروال داخلي sirwaal daakhilee
bring يجلب yajlib
British *adj* بريطاني breetaanee
broken مكسور maksoor
brooch بروش broosh
broom مكنسة miknasa
brother أخ akh
brown بني bunnee
bugs حشرات Hasharaat
building مبنى mabna
burn *n* حرق Harq
bus باص baas
bus station محطة الباص maHatat al-baas
bus stop موقف الباص mohqif al-baas
bus ticket تذكرة للباص tazkara lil-baas
bus tour جولة بالباص johla bil-baas
business أعمال a'aamaal
business card كرت الأعمال kart al-a'aamaal
business center مركز الأعمال markaz al-a'aamaal
business class درجة الأعمال darajat al-a'amaal
business hours أوقات العمل ohqaat al-'amal
busy مشغول mashghool
butcher لحام laHaam
butter زبدة zibdah
buttock ردفين ridfayn
buy *v* يشتري yashtaree
bye مع السلامة ma' al-salaama

C

cabin كابينة kaabeena
cafe مقهى maqha
call (telephone) يتصل yattasil

179

call collect كلفة المكالمة على المتصل kulfat al-mukaalama 'alal-muttasil

calorie حريرات Hurayraat

camera كاميرا kaameera

camera store محل الكاميرات maHal al-kameeraat

camp v يخيم yukhayem

camping stove فرن مخيم furn mukhayam

campsite مخيم mukhayyam

Canada كندا kanada

Canadian كندي kanadee

cancel الغي 'alghi

car سيارة sayaara

car hire [BE] تأجير السيارات ta'ajeer al-sayaraat

car park [BE] موقف السيارات mohkif al-sayaraat

car rental تأجير السيارات ta'ajeer al-sayaraat

car seat مقعد سيارة maq'ad sayaara

carafe إبريق ebreeq

card بطاقة bitaaqa

carry-on (piece of hand luggage) حقيبة يد Haqeebat yad

cart (for luggage, shopping) عربة 'aaraba

carton كرتونة kartoona

cash كاش kaash

cash advance دفعة مسبقة duf'aa musabbaqa

cashier محاسب muHaasib

casino كازينو kazeenoo

castle قلعة qal'a

cave كهف kahf

CD سي دي see dee

cell phone هاتف نقال haatif naqaal

Celsius سلسيوس selseeyoos

centimeter سنتمتر santimeter

certificate شهادة shahaada

chair كرسي kursee

change v **(baby)** يغير حفاض الطفل yughayir Hifaaz al-tifl; n **(money)** يبدل yubaddil; n **(travel)** يغير yughayer

charcoal فحم faHam

charge v **(cost)** يطلب yatlub; n **(cost)** سعر si'r

cheap رخيص rakhees

check (in restaurant) حساب Hisaab; n **(payment)** شيك sheek; v يفحص yafHas; n **(luggage)** يودع الأمتعة yuwadi al-amti'a

check-in إجراءات السفر ejra'aat al-safar

checking account حساب الجاري Hisaab al-jaaree

check-out (from hotel) مغادرة الفندق mughaadarat al-funduq

chemical toilet تواليت كيميائي al-toowaaleet al-kimiyaa'ee

chemist [BE] صيدلية saydaleeya

cheque [BE] شيك sheek

chest صدر sadr

chest pain ألم في الصدر 'alam feel sadr

chewing gum علكة 'ilka

child طفل tifl

children's menu قائمة طعام للأطفال qaa'imat ta'aam lil-atfaal

children's portion وجبات أصغر للأطفال wajabaat asghar lil-atfaal

child's seat كرسي خاص للأطفال kursee khaas lil-atfaal

chopstick عيدان صينية للأكل aydaan seeneeya lil-akl

church كنيسة kaneesa

cigar سيجار seeghaar

cigarette سجائر sijaa'ir

claim form استمارة مطالبة istimaara mutaalaba

class (in school) صف saff

classical music موسيقى كلاسيكية mooseeqa klaaseekeeya

clean adj نظيف nazeef

cleaning supplies مواد تنظيف mawaad tanzeef

cliff منحدر munHadar

cling film [BE] غلاف نايلون ghilaaf nayloon

clock ساعة حائطية saa'a Haa'iteeya

close (near) قريب qareeb; v يغلق yaghliq

closed مغلق mughlaq

clothes ملابس malaabis

clothing store محل الملابس maHal al-malaabis

club نادي naadee

coat معطف mi'ataf

coffee shop مقهى maqha

coin قطعة نقدية qit'aa naqdeeya

colander مصفاة misfaah

cold adj بارد baarid; n (illness) رشح rashH

colleague زميل zameel

cologne كولونيا koloonya

color صبغة sabgha

comb مشط misht

come يأتي ya'atee

complaint شكوى shakwa

computor كومبيوتر kampyootir

concert حفلة موسيقية Hafla mooseeqeeya

concert hall قاعة الحفلات الموسيقية qaa'at al-Haflaat al-mooseeqeeya

conditioner بلسم balsam

condom واقي ذكري waaqee zikree

conference مؤتمر mu'atamar

confirm يؤكد yu'akid

congestion احتقان eHtiqaan

connect يتصل yattasil

connection (travel) تبديل طائرة tabdeel taa'ira; (internet) اتصال ettisaal

constipated مصاب بإمساك musaab bi-emsaak

consulate قنصلية konsooleeya

consultant مستشار mustashaar

contact v يتصل yattasil

contact lens عدسة لاصقة 'aadasa laasiqa

contact lens solution محلول للعدسات اللاصقة maHlool lil-adasaat al-laasiqa

contagious معد mu'din

convention hall قاعة المؤتمرات qaa'at al-mu'atamaraat

cook v يطبخ yatbukh

cooking facilities لوازم طبخ lawaazim tabkh

cooking gas غاز الطبخ gaaz al-tabkh

cool (temperature) بارد قليلاً baarid qaleelan

copper نحاس nuHaas

corkscrew فتاحة النبيذ fataaHat al-nabeez

corner زاوية zaaweeya

cost v يكلف yukalif

cot سرير قابل للطوي sareer qaabil lil-tawwi; [BE] سرير أطفال sareer atfaal

cotton قطن qutn

cough n سعال su'aal

country code رمز البلد ramz al-balad

cover charge رسم الخدمة rasm al-khidma

cramps تشنج tashanuj

crash *n* (in car) حادث اصطدام Haadis estedaam

cream (ointment) مرهم marham

credit ائتمان e'atimaan

credit card بطاقة ائتمان bitaaqat al-e'atimaan

crew neck ياقة مدورة yaaqa mudawwara

crib سرير أطفال sareer atfaal

crystal كريستال kreestaal

cup فنجان finjaan

currency عملة 'umla

currency exchange تبديل العملات tabdeel al-'umlaat

currency exchange office مكتب تبديل العملات maktab tabdeel al-'umlaat

customs الجمرك jumruk

customs declaration form تصريح جمركي tasreeH jumrukee

cut *n* جرح jurH; *v* (hair) يقص yaquss

cute جميل jameel

cycling ركوب الدراجة rukoob al-daraaja

D

dairy منتجات الألبان muntajaat al-albaan

damaged تالف taalif

dance *v* يرقص yarqus

dance club نادي للرقص naadee lil-raqs

dancing الرقص raqs

dangerous خطير Khateer

dark غامق ghaamik

date (on calendar) تاريخ ta'areekh

day يوم yohm

deaf أصم asam

debit سحب من الحساب الجاري saHab min al-Hisaab

deck chair كرسي للشاطئ kursee lil-shaatee'

degrees (temperature) درجات darajaat

delay *n* يتأخر yata'akhar

delete *v* يمحي yamHi

delicatessen محل الأطعمة الفاخرة maHal al-at'ima al-faakhira

delicious لذيذ lazeez

denim جينز jeenz

dentist طبيب أسنان tabeeb asnaan

deodorant مزيل الرائحة muzeel al-raa'iHa

department store محل تجاري maHal tijaaree

departure gate بوابات السفر bawabaat al-safar

departures (airport) مغادرة mughaadara

deposit عربون 'arboon; (at bank) إيداع eedaa'

desert صحراء saHraa'

detergent منظف munazzif

detour تحويلة taHweela

develop (film) تحميض taHmeed

diabetic مريض بالسكري mareed bil-sukaree

dial *v* يضغط yidghut

diamond ألماس almaas

diaper حفاضات Hifaadaat

diarrhea إسهال es-haal

diesel ديزل deezil

182

difficult صعب su'ub
digital دجيتال dijeetaal
digital camera كاميرا دجيتال kaameera dijitaal
digital photo صور دجيتال suwwar dijeetaal
digital print صور دجيتال suwwar dijeetaal
dining room غرفة الطعام ghurfat al-ta'aam
dinner عشاء 'aashaa'
direction اتجاه itijaah
dirty وسخ wisikh
disabled معاق mu'aaq
disabled-accessible [BE] مكان مجهز لاستقبال المعاقين makaan mujahhaz li-esteqbaal al-mu'aaqeen
disabled toilet [BE] تواليت خاص للمعاقين toowaaleet khas lil- mu'aaqeen
disconnect يقطع الاتصال yaqta' al-ettisaal
discount تخفيض takhfeed
dish صحن saHn
dishwasher غسالة الصحون ghasaalat al-suHoon
dishwashing liquid سائل لغسيل الصحون saa'il li-ghaseel al-suHoon
display case فترينا fitreena
disposable موس الحلاقة للاستعمال مرة واحدة moos al-Hilaaqa lil-esti'amaal marra waaHida
dive v يغطس yaghtus
diving equipment معدات الغوص mu'idaat lil-ghats
divorced مطلق mutallaq
dizzy يشعر بدوار yash'ur bl-duwaar
doctor طبيب tabeeb
doll دمية dumya

dollar دولار doolaar
domestic محلي maHalee
door باب baab
dormitory غرفة نوم ghurfat nohm
double bed سرير مزدوج sareer muzdowaj
double room غرفة مزدوجة ghurfa muzdowaja
downtown (direction) باتجاه مركز المدينة bi-ettijah markaz al-madeena
downtown area مركز المدينة markaz al-madeena
dozen دزينة duzeena
dress (woman's) فستان fustaan
dress code لباس مناسب llbaas munaasib
drink n مشروب mashroob; v يشرب yashrab
drink menu قائمة المشروبات mashroobaat
drive v يقود yaqood
driver's license رخصة قيادة rukhsat qeeyaada
drop (of liquid) قطرة qatra
drowsiness خمول khumool
dry cleaner محل تنظيف ألبسة maHal tanzeef albisa
dummy [BE] لهاية lahaaya
during خلال khilaal
duty (customs) رسوم rusoom
duty-free goods بضائع معفية من الضرائب bidaai'aa mo'aafeeya min al-daraa'ib
DVD دي في دي dee vee dee

E

ear أذن uzn
earache ألم في الأذن 'alam feel uzn

early مبكر mu<u>b</u>akkir

earrings حلق <u>H</u>alaq

east شرق sharq

easy سهل <u>s</u>ahil

eat يأكل ya'akul

economy class درجة سياحية <u>da</u>raja siyaHeeya

Egypt مصر musr

Egyptian مصري <u>mus</u>ree

elbow مرفق mirfaq

electric outlet مأخذ كهرباء <u>ma</u>'akhaz kahra<u>baa</u>'

elevator مصعد <u>mis</u>'ad

e-mail بريد إلكتروني ba<u>ree</u>d elek<u>troo</u>nee

e-mail address عنوان الكتروني 'un<u>waa</u>n elek<u>troo</u>nee

emergency ء طوارىء ta<u>waa</u>ri'

emergency exit مخرج الطوارئ <u>makh</u>raj al-ta<u>waa</u>ri'

empty *adj* فارغ <u>faa</u>righ

enamel (jewelry) خزف <u>kha</u>zaf

end *v* ينتهي yan<u>ta</u>hee

engaged خاطب <u>khaa</u>tib

English (language) الانكليزية al-englee<u>zee</u>ya

engrave ينقش yu<u>n</u>qush

enjoy يستمتع yasta<u>mta</u>'

enter يدخل ya<u>d</u>khul

entertainment تسلية tas<u>lee</u>ya

entrance مدخل <u>mad</u>khal

envelope ظرف zarf

epileptic مصاب بداء الصرع mu<u>saab</u> bi-daa' al<u>su</u>ra

equipment معدات mu'i<u>daa</u>t

escalator سلالم كهربائية sa<u>laa</u>lim kahra<u>baa</u>'eeya

e-ticket تذكرة الكترونية <u>ta</u>zkara elek<u>troo</u>neeya

e-ticket check-in إجـراءات السفر للتذاكر الالكترونية ejra'<u>aat</u> al-<u>sa</u>far lil-ta<u>zaa</u>kir al-elek<u>troo</u>neeya

evening مساء ma<u>saa</u>'

excess luggage وزن أمتعة زائد wazn <u>amti</u>'a <u>zaa</u>'id

exchange *v* يبدل yu<u>baddil</u>

exchange fee رسم الصرف rasm al-sarf

exchange rate سعر الصرف si'r al-sarf

excursion رحلة ri<u>H</u>la

exhausted منهك munhak

exit *v* يخرج <u>yakh</u>ruj; *n* خروج khu<u>roo</u>j

expensive غالي <u>ghaa</u>lee

experienced متمرس muta<u>marras</u>

express سريع sa<u>ree</u>'

express bus باص سريع baas sa<u>ree</u>'

express train قطار سريع qi<u>taar</u> sa<u>ree</u>'

extension رقم فرعي raqm far'ee

extra إضافي edaa<u>fee</u>

extra large كبير جداً ka<u>beer jiddan</u>

extract *v* **(tooth)** يخلع <u>yakh</u>laa'

eye عين ayn

F

face وجه <u>wa</u>jah

facial *n* تنظيف الوجه tan<u>zeef</u> al-<u>wa</u>jah

family عائلة <u>'aa</u>'ila

fan (appliance) مروحة <u>mar</u>waHa

far بعيد ba'<u>eed</u>

farm مزرعة <u>maz</u>ra.aa

far-sighted مصاب بمد النظر mu<u>saab</u> bi-madd al-<u>na</u>zar

fast سريع sa<u>ree</u>'a

fast-food place مطعم للوجبات السريعة <u>mat</u>'am lil-wajа<u>baat</u> al-sa<u>ree</u>'a

fat free خال من الدسم khaal min al-dasm

father أب ab

fax فاكس fax

fax number رقم الفاكس raqm al-faks

fee رسم rasm

feed v (baby) يطعم yut'im

ferry معدية mu'adeeya

fever حرارة مرتفعة Haraara murtafi'a

field حقل Haql

fill out (form) يملأ yimla

fill up (tank) يملأ yimla

filling (in tooth) حشوة Hashwa

film (camera) فيلم feelm

fine (good) جيد jayyid; (for breaking law) مخالفة mukhaalafa

finger إصبع esba'

fingernail ظفر zifr

fire حريق Hareeq

fire department الإطفاء etfaa'

fire door مخرج الحريق makhraj al-Hareeq

first أول awwal

first class درجة أولى daraja oola

fit v (clothing) يقيس yaqees

fitting room غرفة القياس ghurfat al-qeeyaas

fix v يصلح yusalliH

fixed-price سعر محدد si'r muHaddad

flashlight فلاش flash

flash photography تصوير بالفلاش tasweer bil-flash

flat (on vehicle) بنشر bunshur

flight رحلة جوية riHla johweeya

floor (underfoot) أرض ard

florist محل الزهور maHal al-zuhoor

flower زهرة zahra

folk music الموسيقى الشعبية mooseeqa al-sha'abeeya

food طعام ta'aam

food processor فرامة faraama

foot قدم qadam

football [BE] كرة القدم kurrat al-qadam

for لـ li-

forecast توقعات الطقس tawaqoo'a al-taqs

forest غابة ghaaba

fork شوكة shohka

form (to fill in) استمارة estimaara

formula (for baby) طعام للرضع ta'aam lil-radaa'

fort حصن Hisn

fountain نافورة naafoora

free مجاني majaanee

freezer فريزر fireezir

friend صديق sadeeq

from من min

frying pan مقلاة miqlaah

full-service خدمة كاملة khedma kaamila

G

game لعبة lu'aba

garage كراج garaaj

garbage bag كيس قمامة kees qamaama

gas بنزين benzeen

gas station محطة البنزين maHatat al-benzeen

gate (at airport) بوابة bawaaba

gel جل gel

generic drug دواء بدون علامة تجارية dawaa' bidooni 'aalaama tijaareeya

get off (a train/bus/subway) ينزل yanzil

gift هدية hadeeya

gift shop محل الهدايا التذكارية maHal al-hadaaya al-tizkaareeya

girl بنت bint

girlfriend صاحبة saaHiba

give يعطي ya'atee

give way [BE] أعط أحقية الطريق aa'te aHaqeeyat al-tareeq

glass (for drink) كأس ka's; **(material)** زجاج zujaaj

glasses نظارات nazaaraat

go يذهب yaz-hab

gold ذهب zahab

golf جولف golf

golf club مضارب غولف madaarib golf

golf course أرض الغولف ard al-golf

good جيد jayyid

goodbye مع السلامة maa' al-salaama

good afternoon مساء الخير masaa' al-khayr

good evening مساء الخير masaa' al-khayr

good morning صباح الخير sabaaH al-khayr

gram غرام gram

grandchild حفيد Hafeed

grandparent جد jadd

gray رمادي ramaadee

green أخضر akhdar

grocery store محل الخضار maHal al-khudaar

groundcloth حصيرة haseera

ground floor الطابق الأرضي al-taabiq al-ardee

ground-floor room غرفة في الطابق الأرضي ghurfa feel-taabiq al-ardee

groundsheet [BE] حصيرة haseera

group مجموعة mujmoo'a

guide دليل daleel

guide (book) كتاب عن المكان kitaab 'an al-makaan

guide dog كلب إرشاد العميان kalb ershaad al-'umyaan

Gulf (Persian) الخليج العربي al-khaleej al-'arabee

gym جيمنازيوم jimnaaziyoom

gynecologist طبيب نسائي tabeeb nisaa'ee

H

hair شعر sha'ar

hairbrush فرشاة الشعر furshaat al-sha'ar

haircut قصة شعر qassat sha'ar

hair dryer مجفف شعر mujaffif sha'ar

hair salon صالون كوافير saaloon kuwaafeer

hairspray مثبت الشعر musabbit al-sha'aar

hairstylist كوافير koowaafeer

half نصف nisf

half-kilo نصف كيلو nisf keelo

hammer مطرقة mitraqa

hand يد yad

handbag [BE] حقيبة يد Haqeebat yad

hand luggage [BE] حقيبة يد Haqeebat yad

handicapped معاق mu'aaq

handicapped-accessible خاص للمعاقين khaas lil- mu'aaqeen

happen يحصل yaHsal

happy سعيد sa'eed

hat قبعة qob'aa

hay fever حمى القش Hummi al-qash

head رأس ra's

headache صداع sudaa'

headphones سماعات sama'aat
health صحة siHHa
health food store محل الأطعمة الصحية maHal al-at'ima al-siheeya
hearing impaired سمعه ضعيف sam'ee da'eef
heart قلب qalb
heart condition قصور في القلب qusoor feel-qalb
heat الحر Hurr
heater سخان sakhaan
heating [BE] تدفئة tadfi'a
hello السلام عليكم al-salaam 'aalaykum
helmet خوذة khouza
help *n* مساعدة musaa'ada
here هنا huna
hi مرحبا marHaban
high عالي 'aalee
high blood pressure ضغط دم مرتفع dughut dam murtafi'a
highchair كرسي عالي kursee 'aalin
highlights (in hair) هاي لايت haay laayt
highway الطريق السريع al-tareeq al-saree'a
hiking boots جزمة مريحة للمشي jazma mareeHa lil-mashi
hill تل till
hire [BE] يستأجر yasta'ajir
hire car [BE] سيارة مستأجرة sayaara musta'ajara
hitchhike طلب توصيل talb tohseel
hold on (telephone) ينتظر yantazir
holiday [BE] إجازه ejaaza
horsetrack طريق للخيول tareeq al-khuyool
hospital مستشفى mustashfa
hostel نزل nuzul

hot ساخن saakhin; **(spicy)** حار Haar
hotel فندق funduq
hour ساعة saa'aa
house بيت bayt
housekeeping services خدمات تنظيف khedmaat tanzeef
how كيف kayf
how much كم الحساب kam al-Hisaab
hug *v* يعانق yu'aaniq
hungry جائع jaa'ea
hurt *v* يؤلم yu'alim
husband زوج zohj

I

ibuprofen إيبوبروفين ibuprofen
ice machine ماكينة ثلج maakeenat talj
icy يوجد جليد yujad jeleed
ID هوية شخصية haweeya shakhseeya
ill [BE] مريض mareed
in في fee
include يشمل yashmal
indoor pool مسبح مسقوف masbaH masqoof
inexpensive غير مكلف ghayr muklif
infected ملتهب multahib
information معلومات ma'aloomaat
information desk استعلامات este'alamaat
insect bite لدغة الحشرات ladghat al-Hasharaat
insect repellent مادة طاردة للحشرات maada taarida lil-Hasharaat
insert *v* يدخل yadkhil
inside الداخل al-daakhil
insomnia أرق 'araq
instant messenger ماسنجر messenger

insulin انسولين insulin
insurance تأمين ta'ameen
insurance card بطاقة تأمين bitaaqat ta'ameen
insurance company شركة التأمين shirkat al-ta'ameen
interesting مثير للاهتمام museer lil-ehtimaam
international دولي doowalee
International Student Card بطاقة طالب دولية bitaaqat taalib doowaleeya
internet إنترنت internet
internet cafe مقهى إنترنت maqhan internet
interpreter مترجم mutarjim
intersection ملتقى الطرق multaqee al-turuq
intestine أمعاء em'aa
introduce يقدم yuqaddim
invoice n محاسبة muHaasaba
Iran إيران eeraan
Iranian إيراني eeraanee
Iraq العراق al-'iraaq
Iraqi عراقي 'iraaqee
Ireland أيرلندا irlanda
Irish أيرلندي irlandee
iron (for clothes) مكواة mikwa
Israel إسرائيل israa'eel

J

jacket جاكيت jaakeet
jar مرطبان martabaan
jaw فك fakk
jazz موسيقى الجاز mooseeqa al-jaaz
jazz club نادي لموسيقى الجاز naadee li-mooseeqa al-jaaz

jeans بنطلون جينز bantaloon jeenz
jet ski جت سكي jet-ski
jeweler محل المجوهرات maHal al-mujoharaat
jewelry مجوهرات mujoharaat
joint (of body) مفصل mifsal
Jordan الأردن al-urdun
Jordanian أردني urdunnee

K

key مفتاح miftaH
key card مفتاح الغرفة miftaH al-ghurfa
key ring حمالة مفاتيح Hamaalat mafaateeH
kiddie pool مسبح للأطفال masbaH lil-atfaal
kidney (in body) كلية kulya
kilo كيلو keelo
kilogram كيلوغرام kilogram
kilometer كيلومتر kilometer
kiss v يبوس yaboos
kitchen مطبخ matbakh
kitchen foil [BE] رقائق المنيوم raqaa'iq aluminyoom
knee ركبة rukba
knife سكين sikeen
Kuwait الكويت al-kuwayt
Kuwaiti كويتي kuwaytee

L

lace تخريم takhreem
lactose intolerant يتحسس من اللاكتوز yataHasas min al-laktooz
lake بحيرة buHayra
large كبير kabeer
last آخر aakhar
late (time) متأخر muta'akhir

188

launderette [BE] محل تنظيف ألبسة بخدمة ذاتية maHal tanzeef albisa bi-khidma zaateeya

laundromat محل تنظيف ألبسة بخدمة ذاتية maHal tanzeef albisa bi-khidma zaateeya

laundry ملابس للغسيل malaabis al-ghaseel

laundry facility مغسلة maghsala

laundry service خدمة غسيل ملابس khedmat ghaseel malaabis

lawyer محامي muHaamee

leather جلد jild

leave v **(deposit)** يترك yatruk; **(go away)** يغادر yughaadir; **(airplane)** تغادر tughaadir

Lebanese لبناني lubnaanee

Lebanon لبنان lubnaan

left (direction) يسار yasaar

leg ساق saaq

lens عدسة 'aadasa

less أقل aqal

lesson درس dars

letter رسالة risaala

library مكتبة maktaba

Libya ليبيا leebiyaa

Libyan ليبي leebee

life boat قارب النجاة qaarib al-najaah

lifeguard منقذ munqiz

life jacket سترة النجاة sitrat al-najaah

lift [BE] مصعد mis'ad

light فاتح faatiH; n ضوء doh; v **(cigarette)** يشعل yash'aal

lightbulb لمبة lamba

lighter ولاعة walaa'a

like v يحب yuHib

line خط khat

linen كتان kataan

lip شفة shiffa

liquor store محل المشروبات الكحولية maHal al-mashroobaat al-kuHooleeya

liter ليتر leetir

little صغير sagheer

live v يعيش ya'eesh

live music موسيقى حية مmooseeqa Haya

liver (in body) كبد kabd

loafers موكاسان mookaasaan

local محلي maHalee

lock n قفل qifl

lock up يقفل yaqful

locker خزانة khazaana

log off يخرج من الإنترنت yakhruj min al-internet

log on يدخل على الإنترنت yadkhul 'alal internet

login دخول dukhool

long طويل taweel

long-sighted [BE] مصاب بمد النظر musaab bi-madd al-nazar

look v يشوف yashoof

loose (fit) واسع waasia'

lose (something) يفقد yafqud

lost تائه taa'eh

lost and found الأمتعة المفقودة al-amti'a al-mafqooda

lost property [BE] الأمتعة المفقودة al-amti'a al-mafqooda

lotion غسول ghasool

love n محبة maHabba; v **(someone)** يحب yuHibb

low منخفض munHafed

low blood pressure ضغط دم منخفض daghut dam munHafed

luggage أمتعة amti'a

luggage cart عربات الأمتعة 'aarabat al-amti'a

luggage locker خـزائن الأمتعة khazeenat al-amti'a
luggage trolley [BE] عربات الأمتعة 'aarabaat al-amti'a
lunch غذاء ghazaa'
lung رئة ri'a
luxury car سيارة فخمة sayaara fakhma

M

magazine مجلة majalla
magnificent جميل جداً jameel jiddan
mail n بريد bareed
mailbox صندوق البريد sundooq al-bareed
mall مركز تجاري markaz tijaaree
man رجل rajul
manager مدير mudeer
manicure منيكور maneekoor
manual (car) بغيار عادي bi-ghiyar 'aadee
map خـريطة khareeta
market سوق sooq
married متزوج mutazawij
mass (in church) قداس qudaas
massage مساج masaaj
match (game) لعبة lu'aba
matches كبريت kibreet
meal وجبة wajba
mean v يعني ya'anee
measuring cup فنجان للعيار finjaan lil-'aayaar
measuring spoon ملعقة للعيار mil'aaqa lil-'aayaar
mechanic ميكانيكي meekaaneekee
medication دواء dawaa'
medicine دواء dawaa'
medium (size) متوسط mutawassit

meet v يلتقي yaltaqee
meeting اجتماع ejtimaa'
meeting room قاعة اجتماعات qaa'at ejtimaa'aat
membership card بطاقة عضوية bitaaqa uzweeya
memory card كرت ذاكرة kart zaakira
mend [BE] يصلح yusalliH
menu قائمة الطعام qaa'imat al-ta'aam
menu of the day طبق اليوم tabaq al-yohm
merge يدخل في السير yadkhul feel-sayr
message رسالة risaala
microwave مايكروويف meekroowayif
microwaveable مناسب للمايكروويف munaasib lil-maykrowayf
midday [BE] منتصف النهار muntasif al-nahaar
midnight منتصف الليل muntasif al-layl
mileage المسافة المقطوعة al-masaafa al-maqtoo'a
mini-bar ميني بار minibaar
minimum age أدنى adna
minute دقيقة daqeeqa
missing مفقود mafqood
mistake خطأ khata'
mobile home بيت متنقل bayt mutaHarrak
mobile phone [BE] هاتف نقال haatif naqaal
moment لحظة laHza
money مال maal
month شهر shahr
mop ممسحة mimsaHa
moped دراجة بمحـرك daraaja bi-muHarik
more أكثر aktar
morning صباح sabaaH

Moroccan مغربي <u>maghree</u>bee
Morocco المغرب al-<u>maghrib</u>
mosque جامع <u>jaame</u>.a
mother أم umm
motion sickness دوار السفر <u>dawaar</u> al-<u>safar</u>
motorboat زورق <u>zohraq</u>
motorcycle دراجة نارية <u>daraaja</u> naa<u>ree</u>ya
motorway [BE] الطريق السريع al-<u>tareeq</u> al-<u>saree</u>.a
mountain جبل <u>jabal</u>
mountain bike دراجة جبلية <u>daraaja</u> jebe<u>lee</u>ya
mousse (hair) موس moos
mouth فم famm
movie فيلم feelm
movie theater صالة سينما <u>saalat</u> <u>seenema</u>
mugging سلب salb
muscle عضلة <u>azla</u>
museum متحف <u>mat-Haf</u>
music موسيقى moo<u>seeqa</u>
music store محل سيديات ma<u>Hal</u> al-moo<u>seeqa</u>
Muslim مسلم <u>muslim</u>

N

nail file مبرد للأظافر <u>mibrad</u> lil-a<u>zaafir</u>
nail salon صالون تجميل sa<u>loon</u> taj<u>meel</u>
name اسم ism
napkin منديل للمائدة man<u>deel</u> lll-<u>maa</u>.lda
nappy [BE] حفاضات Hifaa<u>daat</u>
nationality جنسية jin<u>seeya</u>
nature preserve محمية طبيعية ma<u>Hmeeya</u> tabee.<u>eeya</u>

nauseous يشعر بغثيان <u>yash</u>.ur bi-ghasa<u>yaan</u>
near قريب qareeb
near-sighted مصاب بقصر النظر mu<u>saab</u> bi-qasr al-<u>nazar</u>
neck رقبة <u>ruqba</u>
necklace عقد .uqd
newspaper جريدة ja<u>reeda</u>
next تالي <u>taalee</u>
nice جميل ja<u>meel</u>
night مساء ma<u>saa</u>.
nightclub نادي ليلي <u>naadee</u> <u>laylee</u>
no لا laa
non-alcoholic بدون كحول bi-<u>doonee</u> ku<u>Hool</u>
non-smoking لغير المدخنين li-<u>ghayr</u> al-<u>modakheneen</u>
noon منتصف النهار mun<u>tasif</u> al-na<u>haar</u>
north شمال shi<u>maal</u>
nose أنف anf
not ليس <u>laysa</u>
nothing لا شيء laa shay
notify يخبر <u>yukhbir</u>
now الآن al-.<u>aan</u>
number رقم raqm
nurse ممرض mu<u>marid</u>

O

off (light, TV etc) إيقاف ee<u>qaaf</u>
office مكتب <u>maktab</u>
office hours أوقات العمل oh<u>qaat</u> al-.<u>aamal</u>
off-licence [BE] محل المشروبات الكحولية ma<u>Hal</u> al-mashroo<u>baat</u> al-kuHoo<u>leeya</u>
oil زيت <u>zayit</u>
OK حسناً <u>Hasanan</u>

old قديم qadeem

old town المدينة القديمة al-madeena al-qadeema

Oman عمان 'omaan

Omani عماني omaanee

on (light, TV etc) تشغيل tashgheel

once مرة mara

one واحد waaHid

one-way ذهاب zehaab

only فقط faqat

open v يفتح yaftaH; adj مفتوح maftooH

opposite مقابل muqaabil

optician محل نظارات maHall nazaraat

orange (color) برتقالي burtuqaalee

orchestra أوركسترا oorkeestra

order v يطلب yatlub

outdoor pool مسبح masbaH

outside في الخارج feel khaarij

overheated ساخن أكثر من اللازم saakhin aktar min al-laazim

overlook (scenic place) إطلالة etlaala

overnight طوال الليل tawaal al-layl

oxygen treatment علاج بالأوكسجين 'elaaj bil-ohkseejeen

P

p.m. بعد الظهر ba'ad al-zuhr

pacifier لهّاية lahaaya

package صندوق sundooq

paddling pool [BE] مسبح أطفال masbaH atfaal

pain ألم 'alam

pajamas بيجامة beejaama

palace قصر qasr

Palestine فلسطين filasteen

Palestinian فلسطيني filasteenee

pants بنطلون bantaloon

pantyhose كولون kooloon

paper ورق warq

paper towel مناشف ورقية manaashif warqeeya

paracetamol [BE] سيتامول sitamol

park n حديقة عامة Hadeeqa 'aama; v (car) يصف yasaff

parking موقف mohqif

parking garage موقف mohqif

parking lot موقف سيارات mohqif sayaraat

parking meter عداد الموقف adaad al-mohqif

part (for car) جزء juz'

part-time دوام جزئي dawaam juz'ee

passenger مسافر musaafir

passport جواز سفر jawaaz safar

passport control مراقبة جوازات السفر muraaqabat jawazaat al-safar

password كلمة مرور kalimat muroor

pastry shop محل حلويات maHal Helweeyaat

patch يرقع yuraqi'a

path ممر mamar

pay v يدفع yadfa'

pay phone هاتف عام haatif 'aam

peak n قمة qimma

pearl لؤلؤ loo'loo'

pedestrian crossing [BE] عبور مشاة 'uboor mushah

pedestrian crosswalk عبور مشاة 'uboor mushah

pediatrician طبيب أطفال tabeebat faal

pedicure بديكور bedeekoor

pen قلم qalam

penicillin بنسلين binisileen

penis عضو ذكري azu zikree

perfume عطر 'utr

period (menstruation) عادة شهرية 'aada shahreeya; **(of time)** مدة mudda

petite صغير جدا sagheer jiddan

petrol [BE] بنزين benzeen

petrol station [BE] محطة البنزين maHatat al-benzeen

pewter قصدير qasdeer

pharmacy صيدلية saydaleeya

phone n تلفون tilifoon; v يتصل yattasil

phone call اتصال هاتفي ejraa' ettisaal haatifee

phone card بطاقة تلفونية bitaaqa tilifooneeya

phone number رقم تلفون raqm tilifoon

photocopy نسخة nuskha

photograph صورة soora

picnic area منطقة النزهات mantaqat al-nuz-haat

piece قطعة qit'aa

Pill (contraceptive) حبوب منع الحمل Huboob mana'a al-Haml

pillow مخدة mikhadda

PIN الرقم السري al-raqm al-siree

pink زهري zahree

plan خطة khutta

plane طائرة taa'ira

plastic wrap غلاف نايلون ghilaaf nayloon

plate صحن saHn

platform رصيف raseef; **(at station) [BE]** خط khatt

platinum بلاتين blaateen

play n **(in theater)** مسرحية masraHeeya; v يلعب yal'ab

playground ملعب mal'ab

playpen مكان محاط بالشباك للعب makaan muHaat bil-shubaak lil-la'ab

please من فضلك min fadlak

plunger غاطس ghaatis

point v يشير yushir

poison سم samm

police الشرطة al-shurta

police report تقرير الشرطة taqreer al-shurta

police station مركز الشرطة markaz al-shurta

pond بركة baraka

pool مسبح masbaH

pop music موسيقى البوب mooseeqa al-poop

post [BE] بريد bareed

postbox [BE] صندوق البريد sundooq al-bareed

postcard كرت بوستال kart boostaal

post office البريد bareed

pot وعاء للطبخ wi'aa' lil-tabkh

pottery إناء فخاري 'enaa' fakhaaree

pound (weight) رطل ratl; **(sterling)** جنيه استرليني gunayha esterleenee

pregnant حامل Haamil

prepaid مسبق الدفع musabaq al-dafa'

prescription وصفة طبية wasfa tibeeya

press (clothes) يكبس yikbis

price سعر si'r

print v يطبع yatba'

problem مشكلة mushkila

produce store محل الخضار maHal al-khudaar

pull v يسحب yis-Hab

purple بنفسجي banafsajee

purse حقيبة يد Haqeebat yad

push v يدفع yadfa'

pushchair [BE] عربة أطفال 'aarabat atfaal

pyjamas [BE] بيجامة beejaama

Q

Qatar قطر qatar
Qatari قطري qataree
quality نوعية noh'eeya
question سؤال su'aal
quiet هادئ haadi'

R

racetrack مضمار السباق midmaar
al-sibaaq
racket (sports) مضرب midrab
railway station [BE] محطة القطار
maHatat al-qitaar
rain n مطر matar
raincoat معطف للمطر mi'ataf lil-matar
rainy ممطر mumtir
rap (music) موسيقى الراب mooseeqa
al-raap
rape n اغتصاب eghtisaab
rash n طفح جلدي tafH jildee
razor موس الحلاقة moos al-Hilaaqa
razor blade شفرات الحلاقة shafaraat
al-Hilaaqa
reach (person) يجد yajid
ready جاهز jaahiz
real أصلي aslee
receipt إيصال eesaal
receive v يستقبل yastaqbil
reception استقبال esteqbaal
recharge v يشحن yash-Han
recommend ينصح yansaH
recycling إعادة التصنيع e'aadat
al-tasaanee'
red أحمر aHmar
refrigerator ثلاجة tallaaja
refund n استرداد النقود estirdaad
al-nuqood

region منطقة mantaqa
regular عادي 'aadee
relationship (personal) علاقة 'elaaqa
rent v يستأجر yasta'ajir
rental car سيارة مستأجرة sayaara
musta'ajara
repair v يصلح yusalliH
report v يبلغ عن yuballigh 'an
reservation حجز Hajz
reserve v يحجز yaHjuz
restaurant مطعم mat'am
restroom تواليت tooaleet
retired متقاعد mutaqaa'id
return v يعود ya'ood; n [BE] ذهاب
وعودة zehaab wa-ohda
rib ضلع zala'a
right (correct) صحيح saHeeH;
(direction) يمين yameen
right of way أحقية الطريق aHaqeeyat
al-tareeq
ring n خاتم khaatim
river نهر nahar
road طريق tareeq
road map خريطة طرق khareetat
tuoroq
romantic رومانسي roomaansee
room غرفة ghurfa
room key كرت المفتاح kart
al-miftaH
room service خدمة غرف khedmat
ghuruf
rotary دوار dawaar
round (in game) جولة johla
roundabout [BE] دوار dawaar
round-trip ذهاب وعودة zehaab
wa-ohda
round-trip ticket تذكرة ذهاب و عودة
tazkara zehaab wa-'ohda
route طريق tareeq

rubbish [BE] قمامة qamaama
rubbish bag [BE] أكياس قمامة akyaas qamaama
ruins آثار aasaar

S

sad حزين Hazeen
safe n خزينة khazeena; (not dangerous) آمن aamin; (not in danger) بأمان bi-amaan
sales tax ضريبة dareeba
salty مالح maaliH
same نفس nafs
sandals صندل sandal
sanitary napkin فوط نسائية fuwat nisaa'eeya
sanitary pad [BE] فوط نسائية fuwat nisaa'eeya
Saudi سعودي sa'oodee
Saudi Arabia السعودية al-sa'oodeeya
sauna ساونا saaohna
save حفظ Hafz
savings account حساب المدخرات Hisaab al-mudakharaat
scanner ماسحة maasiHa
scarf لفاح lifaaH
schedule n جدول مواعيد jadwal mawaa'eed
school مدرسة madrassa
scissors مقص miqass
sea بحر baHr
seat مقعد maq'ad
security أمن amn
see يشوف yashoof
sell يبيع yabee'a
self-service خدمة ذاتية khedma zateeya
seminar ندوة nadwa

send يرسل yursil
senior citizen مسنين musinn
separate منفصل munfasil
serious خطير khateer
service خدمة khidma; (in church) صلاة salaat
shampoo شامبو shampoo
shaving cream كريم للحلاقة kreem lil-Hilaaqa
sheet شراشف sharaashif
shirt قميص qamees
shoe store محل الأحذية maHal al-aHzeeya
shoes أحذية aHzeeya
shopping تسوق، tasawooq
shopping area منطقة التسوق mantaqat al-tasawooq
shopping centre [BE] سوق تجاري markaz al-tijaaree
shopping mall سوق تجاري markaz al-tijaaree
short قصير qaseer
shorts شورت shoort
short-sighted [BE] مصاب بقصر النظر musaab bi-qasr al-nazar
shoulder كتف katif
show v يري yuree
shower دش doosh
shrine مزار mazaar
sick مريض mareed
sightseeing tour جولة لزيارة المعالم johla li-ziyaarat al-ma'aalim
sign v يوقع yuwaqe'a
silk حرير Hareer
silver فضة fidda
single عازب 'aazib
single bed سرير مفرد sareer mufrad
single room غرفة مفردة ghurfa mufrada

195

single ticket [BE] تذكرة ذهاب zehaab

sister أخت ukht

sit يجلس yajlis

size قياس qeeyaas

skin جلد jild

skirt تنورة tanoora

sleeping bag حقيبة للنوم Haqeeba lil-nohm

slice شريحة shareeHat

slippers شبشب shibshib

slow بطيء batee'

slowly ببطء bi-but'

small صغير sagheer

smoking للمدخنين lil-modakhineen

snack bar مطعم للوجبات الخفيفة mat'am lil-wajabaat al-khafeefa

sneakers أحذية رياضية aHzeeya reeyaadeeya

snorkeling equipment شنركل shnurkel

snowy يتساقط الثلج yatasaaqat al-talj

soap صابون saaboon

soccer كرة القدم kurrat al-qadam

socks جرابات juraabaat

sold out خلصت التذاكر khalasat al-tazaakir

sore throat ألم الحلق 'alam al-Halq

sorry (apology) آسف aasif

south جنوب janoob

souvenir هدايا تذكارية hadaaya tizkaareeya

souvenir store محل الهدايا التذكارية maHal al-hadaaya al-tizkaareeya

spa سبا spa

sparkling water مياه غازية miyaah ghaazeeya

spatula ملعقة مسطحة mil'aaqa musataHa

speak يتكلم yatakallam

special خاص khaas

specialist *n* أخصائي akhsaa'ee

spicy حار Haar

spine عمود فقري 'amood faqree

spoon ملعقة mil'aaqa

sporting goods store محل الأدوات الرياضية maHal al-adawaat al-reeyaadeeya

sprain *n* التواء في المفصل eltiwaa' feel-mifsal

sprained ملتوي multawee

stadium ملعب mal'ab

stairs درج daraj

stamp *n* طابع taabe'

start *v* يبدأ yabda

station (railroad) محطة muHatta

station wagon سيارة بوكس sayaara boks

stay *v* ينزل yanzil

steal يسرق yasriq

steep شديد الانحدار shadeed al-enHedaar

sterling silver فضة fidda

stolen مسروق masrooq

stomach معدة mi'ada

stomachache ألم في المعدة feel mi'ada

stool (bowel movement) براز biraaz

stop *v* يقف yaqif; *n* (on bus route) موقف mohqif

store directory دليل المحلات التجارية daleel al-maHalaat al-tijaareeya

stove فرن furn

straight مستقيم mustaqeem

straight ahead على طول 'ala tool

strange غريب ghareeb

stream جدول jadwal

street شارع shaare'

stroller عربة أطفال 'aarabat atfaal

student طالب taalib

study v يدرس yadrus
stunning مذهل muz-hil
subway مترو الأنفاق metro al-anfaaq
subway station محطة مترو الأنفاق maHatat metro al-anfaaq
Sudan السودان al-soodaan
Sudanese سوداني soodaanee
suit (clothing) طقم taqm
suitable مناسب munaasib
suitcase حقيبة Haqeeba
sun شمس shams
sunblock واقي شمسي waaqee shamsee
sunburn حروق شمسية Hurooq shamseeya
sunglasses نظارات شمسية nazaaraat shamseeya
sunny مشمس mushmis
sunscreen واقي شمسي waaqee shamsee
sunstroke ضربة شمس darbat shams
super (fuel) ممتاز mumtaaz
supermarket سوبر ماركت soopermarkit
surcharge أجرة إضافية ujra idaafeeya
surfboard لوح لركوب الأمواج looH li-rukoob al-amwaaj
surgical spirit [BE] كحول طبي kuHool tibbee
swallow v يبتلع yabtala'a
sweater كنزة صوف kanzat soof
sweatshirt كنزة رياضة kanzat reeyaada
sweet حلو Helu
sweets [BE] سكاكر sakaakir
swim v يسبح yasbaH
swimsuit مايوه maayoh
Syria سوريا sooriyaa
Syrian سوري sooree

table طاولة taawala
tablet حبة Habba
take v يأخذ ya'akhuz
take off (shoes) يخلع yikhla'
tampon سدادات قطنية للسيدات sadadaat qutneeya lil-sayidaat
taste v يتذوق yatazawaq
taxi تاكسي taksee
tea شاي shay
team فريق fareeq
teaspoon ملعقة صغيرة mil'aaqa
telephone تلفون tilifoon
temple (religious) معبد ma'abad
temporary مؤقت muwaqata
tennis التنس al-tennis
tennis court ملاعب تنس malaa'ib tennis
tent خيمة khayma
tent peg أوتاد الخيمة ohtaad lil-khayma
tent pole عمود الخيمة 'aamood lil-khayma
terminal (airport) تيرمنال terminaal
terrible فظيع fazee'a
text v يبعث اس ام اس yab'as SMS; n اس ام اس SMS
thank you شكراً shukran
that ذلك zaalik
theater مسرح masraH
theft سرقة sirqa
there هناك hunaak
thief لص liss
thigh فخذ fakhz
thirsty عطشان 'atshaan
this هذا haza
throat حلق Halq

thunderstorm عاصفة رعدية 'aasifa ra'adeeya

ticket تذكرة tazkara

ticket office مكتب التذاكر maktab al-tazaakir

tie n كرافيت kraveet

tight (fit) ضيق dayyik

tights [BE] كولون kooloon

time وقت waqt

timetable [BE] جدول مواعيد jadwal mawaa'eed

tire دولاب doolaab

tired تعبان ta'abaan

tissue مناديل ورقية manaadeel warqeeya

to إلى ila

tobacconist كشك الجرائد kushk al-sijaa'ir

today اليوم al-yohm

toe إصبع القدم esba' al-qadam

toenail ظفر إصبع القدم zifr esba' al-qadam

toilet [BE] تواليت toowaaleet

toilet paper ورق تواليت warq toowaaleet

toll road طريق برسم مرور tareeq bi-rasm muroor

tomorrow غداً ghadan

tonight الليلة al-layla

too (also) أيضاً aydan; **(excessively)** أكثر من اللازم aktar min al-laazim

tooth سن sinn

toothache ألم في الأسنان 'alam feel asnaan

toothbrush فرشاة أسنان furshaat asnaan

toothpaste معجون أسنان ma'aajoon asnaan

torch [BE] بيل beel

total (amount) مُجمل mujmal

tour جولة johla

tourist سائح sayaaH

tourist information office مكتب الاستعلامات السياحية maktab al-este'alamaat al-seeyaaHeeya

tow truck شاحنة قاطرة shaaHina qaatira

towel منشفة minshafa

tower برج burj

town مدينة madeena

town hall البلدية baladeeya

town map خريطة المدينة khareetat al-madeena

town square ساحة المدينة saaHat al-madeena

toy لعبة أطفال lu'abat atfaal

toy store محل ألعاب الأطفال maHal al'aab al-atfaal

track (for trains) خط khatt

traditional تقليدي taqleedee

traffic circle دوار dawaar

traffic light إشارة مرور eshaarat muroor

trail ممر mamar

trailer عربة مقطورة 'aaraba maqtoora

train n قطار qitaar

train station محطة قطار maHatat qitaar

transfer v (traveling) يبدل yughayer

translate يترجم yutarjim

trash قمامة qamaama

travel agency مكتب سياحة و سفر maktab safar

travelers check شيك سياحي sheek seeyaaHee

traveller's cheque [BE] شيك سياحي sheek seeyaaHee

travel sickness [BE] دوار السفر dawaar al-safar

tree شجرة shajra
trim (haircut) تطريف شعر tatreef sha'ar
trip رحلة riHla
trolley [BE] عربة 'aaraba
trousers [BE] بنطلون bantaloon
T-shirt تي شيرت tee sheert
tumble dry يعصر في الغسالة yu'asar feel ghasaala
Tunisia تونس toonis
Tunisian تونسي toonisee
turn off (light) يطفئ yat'fa'
turn on (light) يشعل yash'al
TV تلفزيون televiziyoon
tyre [BE] دولاب doolaab

U

ugly بشع bashe'a
umbrella مظلة mazalla
underground [BE] مترو الأنفاق metro al-anfaaq
underground station [BE] محطة مترو الأنفاق maHatat metro al-anfaaq
underpants [BE] سروال داخلي sirwaal daakhilee
understand يفهم yafham
underwear ملابس داخلية malaabis dakhileeya
United Kingdom بريطانيا breetaaneeya
United States أمريكا amreeka
unleaded بدون رصاص bi-dooni rasaas
unlimited mileage بأميال غير محدودة amyaal ghayr maHdooda
urgent مستعجل musta'ajil
urine بول bool
use v يستخدم yastakhdim

username اسم المستخدم ism al-mustakhdim
utensil أدوات الطبخ adawaat al-tabkh

V

vacation إجازة ejaaza
vacuum cleaner مكنسة كهربائية miknasa kahraba'eeya
vagina مهبل mahbil
vaginal infection التهاب مهبلي eltihaab mahbalee
valley وادي waadee
value n قيمة qeema
van فان van
VAT [BE] ضريبة dareeba
vegan لا يأكل المنتجات الحيوانية laa akul al-muntajaat al-Haywaaneeya
vegetarian نباتي nabaatee
vehicle registration تسجيل سيارة tasjeel sayaara
vending machine ماكينة بيع maakeenat bee'a
very جداً jiddan
viewpoint [BE] إطلالة etlaala
visit v يزور yazoor
visiting hours مواعيد الزيارة mawaa'eed al-ziyaara
visually impaired نظره ضعيف nazarhu da'eef
volleyball كرة الطائرة kurrat al-taa'ira
vomiting أيتقيأ yataqaya'

W

wait v ينتظر yantazar
waiter غرسون gharsoon
waiting room غرفة انتظار ghurfat intizaar
waitress آنسة aanisa

wake (person) يوقظ yohqiz

wake-up call مكالمة إيقاظ mukaalamat eeqaaz

walk n نزهة nuz-ha

walking route طرق السير turuq al-sayr

wallet محفظة miHfaza

warm دافئ daafi'; v يسخن yusakhin

wash v يغسل yughassal

washing machine غسالة الملابس ghasaalat al-malaabis

washing-up liquid [BE] سائل للجلي saa'il lil-jalli

watch n ساعة يد saa'at yad

water ماء maa'

waterfall شلال shalaal

water skis ألواح للتزحلق على الماء alwaaH lil-tazaHluq 'alal-maa'

weather طقس taqs

week أسبوع usboo'

weekend عطلة نهاية الأسبوع 'utlat nihaayat al-'usboo'

weekly أسبوعي usboo'ee

well-rested مرتاح murtaaH

west غرب gharb

what ماذا maaza

wheelchair كرسي المقعدين kursee al-muq'aadeen

wheelchair ramp منحدر خاص لكرسي المقعدين munHadir khaas li-kursee al-muq'aadeen

when متى mata

where أين ayn

where to إلى أين ila ayn

which أي ay

white أبيض abyad

white gold ذهب أبيض zahab abyad

who مَن man

widowed أرمل armal

wife زوجة zohja

window نافذة naafiza

window seat مقعد على النافذة maq'ad 'alal-naafiza

windsurfer لوح شراعي looH shiraa'ee

wine list قائمة النبيذ qaa'imat al-nabeez

wireless internet إنترنت لاسلكي internet laasilkee

wireless internet service خدمة إنترنت لاسلكي khedmat internet laasilkee

with مع ma'

withdraw يسحب yas-Hab

without بدون bi-doon

woman امرأة imra'a

wool صوف soof

work v يعمل ya'amal

wrist معصم mi'asam

write (down) يكتب yuktub

Y

year سنة sana

yellow أصفر asfar

yellow gold ذهب أصفر zahab asfar

Yemen اليمن al-yaman

Yemeni يمني yamanee

yes نعم na'am

yesterday البارحة umbaariH

yield (in traffic) أعط أحقية الطريق 'aa'te aHaqeeyat al-tareeq

yogurt لبن labn

young شاب shaab

you're welcome عفواً 'aafwan

youth hostel بيت شباب bayt shebaab

Z

zoo حديقة الحيوانات Hadeeqat al-Hayawanaat

Arabic–English Dictionary

A

a'aamaal أعمال business

'aada shahreeya عادة شهرية period (menstruation)

'aadasa عدسة lens

'aadasa laasiqa عدسة لاصقة contact lens

'aadee عادي regular

'aadeem al-nuk-ha عديم النكهة bland (food)

'aafwan عفواً that's ok

'aa'ila عائلة family

aakhar آخَر another

aakher آخِر last

'aalaykum عليكم hello

'aalee عالي high

aamin آمِن safe (not dangerous)

'aamood lil-khayma عمود الخيمة tent pole

aanisa آنسة waitress

'aaraba عربة cart [trolley BE]

'aaraba maqtoora عربة مقطورة trailer

'aarabat al-amti'a عربات الأمتعة luggage cart [trolley BE]

'aarabat atfaal عربة أطفال stroller [pushchair BE]

'aarabee عربي Arab, Arabic; al-'aarabeeya العربية Arabic (language)

'aarboon عربون deposit

'aard baalay عرض باليه ballet

'aard oobira عرض أوبرا opera

aasaar آثار ruin

'aaseer عصير juice

'aashaa' عشاء dinner

aasif آسف sorry

'aasifa ra'adeeya عاصفة رعدية thunderstorm

'aa'te aHaqeeyat al-tareeq أعط أحقية الطريق yield [give way BE]

'aayd meelaad عيد ميلاد birthday

'aazib عازب single

ab أب father

abyad أبيض white

adaad al-mohqif عداد الموقف parking meter

adawaat al-tabkh أدوات الطبخ utensil

adna 'umr أدنى عمر minimum age

afdal أفضل better

ahalan wa sahlan أهلاً و سهلاً you're welcome

aHaqeeyat al-tareeq أحقية الطريق right of way

aHmar أحمر red

aHsan أحسن best

aHzeeya أحذية shoes

aHzeeya reeyaadeeya أحذية رياضية sneakers

AIDS أيدز AIDS

akh أخ brother

akhdar أخضر green

akhsaa'ee أخصائي specialist n

aktar أكثر more

aktar min al-laazim أكثر من اللازم excessively, too

akyaas qamaama أكياس قمامة garbage bag [bin bag BE]

'ala tool على طول straight ahead
al-'aan الآن now
'alam ألم pain
'alam al-Halq ألم الحلق sore throat
'alam feel asnaan ألم في الأسنان toothache
'alam feel mi'ada ألم في المعدة stomachache
'alam feel sadr ألم في الصدر chest pain
'alam feel uzn ألم في الأذن earache
'alam feel zuhr ألم في الظهر backache
al-amti'a al-mafqooda الأمتعة المفقودة lost and found [lost property BE]
albaariHa البارحة yesterday
'alghi الغي cancel
al-khaleej al-'arabee الخليج العربي Gulf (Persian)
al-layla الليلة tonight
almaas الماس diamond
alwaaH lil-tazaHluq 'alal-maa' ألواح للتزحلق على الماء water ski
al-yohm اليوم today
amn أمن security
'amood faqree عمود فقري spine
amreeka أمريكا United States
amreekaanee أمريكي American
amti'a أمتعة luggage
anf أنف nose
aqal أقل less
'araq أرق insomnia
'arboon عربون deposit
ard أرض floor
ard al-golf أرض الغولف golf course
armal أرمل widowed
asam أصم deaf
asbireen أسبرين aspirin

asfar أصفر yellow
aslee أصلي real
aswad أسود black
atar jaanibee آثار جانبية side effect
'atshaan عطشان thirsty
awwal أول first
ay أي which
ay shay أي شيء anything
aydan أيضاً too (also)
'ayn عين eye
ayn أين where
azla عضلة muscle
'azm عظم bone
azraq أزرق blue
azu zikree عضو ذكري penis

B

baab باب door
ba'ad بعد after
ba'ad al-zuhr بعد الظهر afternoon, p.m.
baar بار bar
baarid بارد cold *adj*
baarid qaleelan بارد قليلاً cool (temperature)
baas باص bus
baas saree' باص سريع express bus
ba'eed بعيد far
baHr بحر sea
baHraynee بحريني Bahraini; al-baHrayn البحرين Bahrain
baladeeya البلدية town hall
balsam بلسم conditioner
banafsajee بنفسجي purple
bank بنك bank
bantaloon بنطلون pants [trousers BE]
bantaloon jeenz بنطلون جينز jeans
baraka بركة pond

bareed بريد mail *n* [post BE], post office

bareed elektroonee بريد إلكتروني e-mail

baseball بيسبول baseball

bashe'a بشع ugly

bataareeya بطارية battery

bataneeya بطانية blanket

batee' بطيء slow

bawaaba بوابة gate (at airport)

bawabaat al-safar بوابات السفر departure gate

bayj بيج beige

bayt بيت house

bayt mutaHarrak بيت متنقل mobile home

bayt shebaab بيت شباب youth hostel

bedeekoor بديكور pedicure

beejaama بيجامة pajamas [pyjamas BE]

beel بيل flashlight [torch BE]

benzeen بنزين gas [petrol BE]

bi-amaan بأمان safe, not in danger

bi-but' ببطء slowly

bidaai'aa lil-e'aalaan 'aanha بضائع للإعلان عنها goods to declare

bidaai'aa mo'aafeeya min al-daraa'ib بضائع معفية من الضرائب duty-free goods

bi-doon بدون without

bi-dooni rasaas بدون رصاص unleaded

bi-ettijah markaz al-madeena باتجاه مركز المدينة downtown

bi-ghiyar 'aadee بغيار عادي manual (car)

bi-munfaridih بمفرده alone

binisileen بنسلين penicillin

bint بنت girl

biraaz براز stool (bowel movement)

bitaaqa بطاقة card

bitaaqa tilifooneeya بطاقة تلفونية phone card

bitaaqa uzweeya بطاقة عضوية membership card

bitaaqat e'atimaan بطاقة ائتمان credit card

bitaaqat su'ood بطاقة صعود boarding pass

bitaaqat taalib doowaleeya بطاقة طالب دولية International Student Card

bitaaqat ta'ameen بطاقة تأمين insurance card

blaateen بلاتين platinum

blooza بلوزة blouse

bool بول urine

breetaanee بريطاني British *adj*

breetaaneeya بريطانيا United Kingdom

broosh بروش brooch

buHayra بحيرة lake

bunnee بني brown

bunshur بنشر flat (on vehicle)

burj برج tower

burtuqaal برتقال orange (fruit)

burtuqaalee برتقالي orange (color)

D

daafi' دافئ warm

daakhil داخل inside

daleel دليل guide

daleel al-maHalaat al-tijaareeya دليل المحلات التجارية store directory

dam دم blood

damaad ضمادات bandage

daqeeqa دقيقة minute

daraaja دراجة bicycle

daraaja bi-muHarik دراجة بمحرك
moped

daraaja jebeleeya دراجة جبلية
mountain bike

daraaja naareeya دراجة نارية
motorcycle

daraj دَرَج stair

daraja oola درجة أولى first class

daraja siyaHeeya درجة سياحية
economy class

darajaat درجات degrees
(temperature)

darajat al-a'amaal درجة الأعمال
business class

darbat shams ضربة شمس sunstroke

dareeba ضريبة sales tax [VAT BE]

dars درس lesson

dawaa' دواء medication, medicine

dawaa' bidooni 'aalaama
tijaareeya دواء بدون علامة تجارية
generic drug

dawaam juz'ee دوام جزئي part-time

dawaar دوار traffic circle [roundabout
BE]

dawaar al-safar دوار السفر motion
[travel BE] sickness

dayyik ضيق tight (fit)

dee vee dee دي في دي DVD

deezil ديزل diesel

dijeetaal ديجيتال digital

doh ضوء light n

doolaab دولاب tire [tyre BE]

doolaar دولار dollar

doosh دُش shower

doowalee دولي international

duf'aa musabbaqa دفعة مسبقة cash
advance

dughut dam munHafed ضغط دم
منخفض low blood pressure

dughut dam murtafi'a ضغط دم مرتفع
high blood pressure

dukhool دخول login

dumya دمية doll

duzeena دزينة dozen

E

e'aadat al-tasaanee' إعادة التصنيع
recycling

e'atidaa' اعتداء attack

e'atimaan ائتمان credit

ebreeq إبريق carafe

edaafee إضافي extra

eedaa' إيداع deposit (at bank)

eeqaaf إيقاف off

eeraan إيران Iran

eeraanee إيراني Iranian

eesaal إيصال receipt

eghtisaab اغتصاب rape n

eHtiqaan احتقان congestion

ejaaza إجازة vacation [holiday BE]

ejra'aat al-safar إجراءات السفر check-in

ejra'aat al-safar lil-tazaakir
al-elektroneeya إجراءات السفر
للتذاكر الالكترونية e-ticket check-in

ejtimaa' اجتماع meeting

'elaaj aroomaatee علاج أروماتي
aromatherapy

'elaaj bil-ibar علاج بالإبر acupuncture

'elaaj bil-ohkseejeen علاج بالأوكسجين
oxygen treatment

'elaaqa علاقة relationship (personal)

eltihaab mafaasil التهاب مفاصل
arthritis

eltihaab mahbalee التهاب مهبلي
vaginal infection

eltiwaa' feel-mifsal التواء في المفصل
sprain n

em'aa أمعاء intestine

'enaa' fakhaaree إناء فخاري pottery

engleezee إنكليزي English; al-engleezeeya الانكليزية English (language)

eqtiHaam اقتحام break-in

esba' إصبع finger

esba' al-qadam إصبع القدم toe

es-haal إسهال diarrhea

eshaarat al-muroor إشارة المرور traffic light

este'alamaat استعلامات information (telephone) [directory enquiries BE], information desk

estelaam al-Haqaa'ib استلام الحقائب baggage claim

esteqbaal استقبال reception

estimaara استمارة form (to fill in)

estirdaad al-nuqood استرداد النقود refund n

etfaa' إطفاء fire department

etlaala إطلالة overlook (scenic place) [viewpoint BE]

ettisaal اتصال connection

ettisaal haatifee اتصال هاتفي phone call

F

faarigh فارغ empty adj

faatiH فاتح light

faHam فحم charcoal

fakhz فخذ thigh

fakk فك jaw

famm فم mouth

faqat فقط only

faraama فرامة food processor

faraamil فرامل brake

fareeq فريق team

fataaHat al-nabeez فتاحة النبيذ corkscrew

fataaHat zujajaat فتاحة زجاجات bottle opener

fax فاكس fax

fazee'a فظيع terrible

fee في in

feel-khaarij في الخارج outside

feelm فيلم movie, film (camera)

feel-subH في الصبح a.m.

fidda فضة silver

filasteen فلسطين Palestine

filasteenee فلسطيني Palestinian

finjaan فنجان cup

finjaan lil-'aayaar فنجان للعيار measuring cup

fireezir فريزر freezer

fitreena فترينا display case

flash فلاش flashlight [torch BE]

funduq فندق hotel

furn فرن stove

furn mukhayam فرن مخيم camping stove

furshaat al-sha'ar فرشاة الشعر hairbrush

furshaat asnaan فرشاة أسنان toothbrush

fustaan فستان dress (woman's)

futoor فطور breakfast

fuwat nisaa'eeya فوط نسائية sanitary napkins [sanitary pads BE]

G

gaaz al-tabkh غاز الطبخ cooking gas

garaaj كراج garage

gel جل gel

ghaaba غابة forest

ghaalee غالي expensive

ghaamik غامق dark

ghadan غداً tomorrow

gharb غرب west

ghareeb غريب strange

gharsoon غرسون waiter

ghasaalat al-malaabis غسالة الملابس washing machine

ghasaalat al-suHoon غسالة الصحون dishwasher

ghasool غسول lotion

ghayr mashghool غير مشغول available

ghayr muklif غير مكلف inexpensive

ghazaa' غذاء lunch

ghurfa غرفة room

ghurfa feel taabiq al-ardee غرفة في الطابق الأرضي ground-floor room

ghurfa mufrada غرفة مفردة single room

ghurfa muzdowaja غرفة مزدوجة double room

ghurfat intizaar غرفة انتظار waiting room

ghurfat nohm غرفة نوم dormitory

ghurfat qeeyaas غرفة قياس fitting room

ghurfat ta'aam غرفة طعام dining room

golf الغولف golf

gram غرام gram

gunay esterleenee جنيه استرليني pound (sterling)

H

haadi' هادئ quiet

Haadis حادث accident

Haadis estedaam حادث اصطدام crash n (in car)

Haamil حامل pregnant

Haar حار hot (spicy)

haatif 'aam هاتف عام pay phone

haatif naqaal هاتف نقال cell [mobile BE] phone

haay laayt هاي لايت highlights (in hair)

Habba حبة tablet

hadaaya tizkaareeya هدايا تذكارية souvenir

Hadeeqa 'aama حديقة عامة park n

Hadeeqat al-Hayawanaat حديقة الحيوانات zoo

Hadeeqat al-nabataat حديقة النباتات botanical garden

hadeeya هدية gift

Hafeed حفيد grandchild

Hafla mooseeqeeya حفلة موسيقية concert

Hafz حفظ save

Hajz حجز reservation

Halaal حلال halal

Halaaq rijaalee حلاق رجالي barber

Halaq حلق earrings

Halq حلق throat

Hamaalat mafaateeH حمالة مفاتيح key ring

Hamaalat sadr حمالة صدر bra

Hamaam حمام bathroom

Haqeeba حقيبة suitcase

Haqeeba lil-nohm حقيبة للنوم sleeping bag

Haqeebat yad حقيبة يد carry-on [hand luggage BE]

Haqeebat yad حقيبة يد purse [handbag BE]

Haqeebat zuhr حقيبة ظهر backpack

Haql حقل field

Haraara murtafi'a حرارة مرتفعة fever

Hareeq حريق fire

Hareer حرير silk

Harq حرق burn *n*

Hasanan حسناً OK

haseera حصيرة groundcloth [groundsheet BE]

Hasharaat حشرات bug

Hashwa حشوة filling (in tooth)

haweeya shakhseeya هوية شخصية ID

Haywaan حيوان animal

haza هذا this

Hazeen حزين sad

Helu حلو sweet

Hezaam حزام belt

Hifaadaat حفاضات diaper [nappy BE]

Hisaab حساب account; bill; check (in restaurant)

Hisaab al-jaaree حساب الجاري checking account

Hisaab al-mudakharaat حساب المدخرات savings account

Hisn حصن fort

Huboob mana'a al-Haml حبوب منع الحمل Pill (contraceptive)

Hummi al-qash حمى القش hay fever

huna هنا here

hunaak هناك there

Hurayraat حريرات calorie

Hurooq shamseeya حروق شمسية sunburn

Hurr حر heat

I

ila إلى to

ila ayn إلى اين where to

'ilka علكة chewing gum

imra'a امرأة woman

insulin انسولين insulin

internet إنترنت internet

internet laasilkee إنترنت لاسلكي wireless internet

'iraaqee عراقي Iraqi; **al-'iraaq** العراق Iraq

irlanda أيرلندا Ireland

irlandee أيرلندي Irish

ism اسم name

ism al-mustakhdim اسم المستخدم username

israa'eel إسرائيل Israel

istimaara mutaalaba استمارة مطالبة claim form

itijaah اتجاه direction

J

jaa'ea جائع hungry

jaahiz جاهز ready

jaakeet جاكيت jacket

jaame'a جامع mosque

jabal جبل mountain

jadd جد grandparent

jadwal جدول stream

jadwal mawaa'eed جدول مواعيد schedule [timetable BE]

jameel جميل beautiful, nice, cute

jameel jiddan جميل جداً magnificent

janoob جنوب south

jareeda جريدة newspaper

jawaaz safar جواز سفر passport

jayyid جيد fine, good

jazaab جذاب attractive (person)

jazaa'iree جزائري Algerian; **al-jazaa'ir** الجزائر Algeria

jazma جزمة boot

jazma mareeHa lil-mashi جزمة مريحة للمشي hiking boot

jeenz جينز denim

jet-ski جت سكي jet ski

jiddan جداً very

jild جلد leather, skin
jimnaaziyoom جيمنازيوم gym
jinseeya جنسية nationality
jisr جسر bridge
jisr munkhafed جسر منخفض low bridge
johla جولة round (in game), tour
johla bil-baas جولة بالباص bus tour
johla li-ziyaarat al-ma'aalim جولة لزيارة المعالم sightseeing tour
jumruk جمرك customs
juraabaat جرابات sock
jurH جرح cut *n*
juz' جزء part (for car)

K

kaabeena كابينة cabin
kaaHil كاحل ankle
kaameera كاميرا camera
kaameera dijitaal كاميرا دجيتال digital camera
kaash كاش cash
kabd كبد liver (in body)
kabeer كبير big
kabeer jiddan كبير جداً extra large
kahf كهف cave
kalb ershaad al-'umyaan كلب إرشاد العميان guide dog
kalimat al-muroor كلمة مرور password
kam al-Hisaab كم الحساب how much
kampyootir كومبيوتر computer
kanada كندا Canada
kanadee كندي Canadian
kaneesa كنيسة church
kanzat reeyaada كنزة رياضة sweatshirt
kanzat soof كنزة صوف sweater

kart al-a'aamaal كرت الأعمال business card
kart al-miftaH كرت المفتاح room key
kart boostaal كرت بوستال postcard
kart zaakira كرت ذاكرة memory card
kartoona كرتونة carton
ka's كأس glass (for drink)
kataan كتان linen
katif كتف shoulder
kayf كيف how
kazeenoo كازينو casino
keelo كيلو kilo
kees كيس bag
kees qamaama كيس قمامة garbage bag [bin bag BE]
khaal min al-dasm خال من الدسم fat free
khaas خاص special
khaas lil-mu'aaqeen خاص للمعاقين handicapped-accessible
khaatib خاطب engaged
khaatim خاتم ring *n*
khalaat خلاط blender
khalasat al-tazaakir خلصت التذاكر sold out
khalf خلف behind
khareeta خريطة map
khareetat al-madeena خريطة المدينة town map
khareetat tuoroq خريطة طرق road map
khat خط line
khata' خطأ mistake
khateer خطير dangerous, serious
khatt خط track (for train) [platform BE]
khayma خيمة tent
khazaana خزانة locker
khazaf خزف enamel

khazeena خزينة safe *n*

khazeenat al-amti'a خزائن الأمتعة luggage locker

khedma kaamila خدمة كاملة full-service

khedma zateeya خدمة ذاتية self-service

khedmaat tanzeef خدمات تنظيف housekeeping service

khedmat ghaseel malaabis خدمة غسيل ملابس laundry service

khedmat ghuruf خدمة غرف room service

khedmat internet laasilkee خدمة إنترنت لاسلكى wireless internet service

khidma خدمة service

khilaal خلال during

khouza خوذة helmet

khumool خمول drowsiness

khurooj خروج exit

khutoot johweeya خطوط جوية airline

khutta خطة plan

kibreet كبريت matches

kilogram كيلوغرام kilogram

kilometer كيلومتر kilometer

kitaab كتاب book

kitaab 'an al-makaan كتاب عن المكان guide book

koloonya كولونيا cologne

konsooleeya قنصلية consulate

kooloon كولون pantyhose [tights BE]

koowaafeer كوافير hairstylist

korn flayks كورن فلكس cereal

kraveet كرافيت lie *n*

kreem lil-Hilaaqa كريم للحلاقة shaving cream

kreem mu'aaqim كريم معقم antiseptic cream

kreestaal كريستال crystal

kuHool tibbee كحول طبي rubbing alcohol [surgical spirit BE]

kulfat al-mukaalama 'alal-muttasil كلفة المكالمة على المتصل call collect

kulya كلية kidney (in body)

kurrat al-qadam كرة القدم soccer [football BE]

kurrat al-silla كرة السلة basketball

kurrat al-taa'ira كرة الطائرة volleyball

kursee كرسي chair

kursee 'aalin كرسي عالي highchair

kursee al-muq'aadeen كرسي المقعدين wheelchair

kursee khaas lil-atfaal كرسي خاص للأطفال child's seat

kursee lil-shaatee' كرسي للشاطئ deck chair

kushk al-sijaa'ir كشك الجرائد tobacconist

kuwaytee كويتي Kuwaiti; **al-kuwayt** الكويت Kuwait

L

laa لا no

laa shay لا شيء nothing

laaHiqan لاحقاً later

ladghat al-Hasharaat لدغة الحشرات insect bite

laHaam لحام butcher

lahaaya لهّاية pacifier [dummy BE]

laHza لحظة moment

lamba لمبة lightbulb

lawaazim tabkh لوازم طبخ cooking facility

laysa ليس not

lazeez لذيذ delicious

leebee ليبي Libyan

leebiyaa ليبيا Libya

leetir ليتر liter

li- لـ for

libaas munaasib لباس مناسب dress code

lifaaH لفاح scarf

li-ghayr al- modakheneen لغير المدخنين non-smoking

lil-esti'amaal marra waaHida للاستعمال مرة واحدة disposable

lil-modakhineen للمدخنين smoking

lisaan لسان tongue

liss لص thief

looH li-rukoob al-amwaaj لوح لركوب الأمواج surfboard

looH shiraa'ee لوح شراعي windsurfer

loo'loo' لؤلؤ pearl

lu'aba لعبة game

lu'aba لعبة match (game)

lu'abat atfaal لعبة أطفال toy

lubnaan لبنان Lebanon

lubnaanee لبناني Lebanese

M

ma' مع with

ma' al-salaama مع السلامة goodbye

maa' ماء water

maa' saakhin ماء ساخن hot water

maa za ماذا what

ma'aajoon asnaan معجون أسنان toothpaste

ma'abad معبد temple (religious)

maada taarida lil-Hasharaat مادة طاردة للحشرات insect repellent

maakeenat bee'a ماكينة بيع vending machine

maakeenat talj ماكينة ثلج ice machine

ma'akhaz kahrabaa' مأخذ كهرباء electric outlet

maal مال money

maaliH مالح salty

ma'aloomaat معلومات information

maasiHa ماسحة scanner

maayoh مايوه swimsuit

mabna مبنى building

madaarib golf مضارب غولف golf club

madeena مدينة town

madeena qadeema مدينة قديمة old town

madeenat al-malaahee مدينة الملاهي amusement park

madkhal مدخل access, entrance

madrassa مدرسة school

mafqood مفقود missing

maftooH مفتوح open *adj*

maghribee مغربي Moroccan; **al-maghrib** المغرب Morocco

maghsala مغسلة laundry facility

maHaarim lil-tifl محارم للطفل baby wipe

maHabba محبة love *n*

maHal al'aab al-atfaal محل ألعاب الأطفال toy store

maHal al-adawaat al-reeyaadeeya محل الأدوات الرياضية sporting goods store

maHal al-aHzeeya محل الأحذية shoe store

maHal al-antikaat محل الأنتيكات antiques store

maHal al-at'ima al-siheeya محل الأطعمة الصحية health food store

maHal al-hadaaya al-tizkaareeya محل الهدايا التذكارية gift shop, souvenir store

maHal al-kameeraat محل الكاميرات camera store

maHal al-khudaar محل الخضار grocery store

maHal al-malaabis محل الملابس clothing store

maHal al-mashroobaat al-kuHooleeya محل المشروبات الكحولية liquor store [off-licence BE]

maHal al-mooseeqa محل سيديات music store

maHal al-mujoharaat محل المجوهرات jeweler

maHal al-zuhoor محل الزهور florist

maHal Helweeyaat محل الحلويات pastry shop

maHal nazaraat محل نظارات optician

maHal tanzeef albisa محل تنظيف ألبسة dry cleaner

maHal tanzeef albisa bi-khidma zaateeya محل تنظيف ألبسة بخدمة ذاتية laundromat [launderette BE]

maHal tijaaree محل تجاري department store

maHalee محلي domestic

maHalee محلي local

maHatat al-baas محطة الباص bus station

maHatat al-benzeen محطة البنزين gas [petrol BE] station

maHatat al-qitaar محطة القطار train station

maHatat metro al-anfaaq محطة مترو الأنفاق subway [underground BE] station

mahbil مهبل vagina

maHlool lil-adasaat al-laasiqa محلول للعدسات اللاصقة contact lens solution

maHmeeya tabee'eeya محمية طبيعية nature preserve

majaanee مجاني free

majalla مجلة magazine

makaan muHaat bil-shubaak lil-la'ab مكان محاط بالشباك للعب playpen

makaan mujahhaz li-esteqbaal al-mu'aaqeen مكان مجهز لاستقبال المعاقين handicapped- [disabled-BE] accessible

makhbaz مخبز bakery

makhraj مخرج exit

makhraj al-Hareeq مخرج الحريق fire door

makhraj al-tawaari' مخرج الطوارئ emergency exit

maksoor مكسور broken

maktab مكتب office

maktab al-este'alamaat al-seeyaaHeeya مكتب الاستعلامات السياحية tourist information office

maktab al-tazaakir مكتب التذاكر ticket office

maktab safar مكتب سياحة و سفر travel agency

maktab tabdeel al-'umlaat مكتب تبديل العملات currency exchange office

maktaba مكتبة bookstore, library

malaabis ملابس clothes

malaabis dakhileeya ملابس داخلية underwear

malaabis lil ghaseel ملابس للغسيل laundry (clothes)

211

malaa'ib al-tennis ملاعب تنس tennis court

mal'ab ملعب playground, stadium

mamar ممر path, trail

mamzooj بيض ممزوج scrambled

man من who

manaadeel warqeeya مناديل ورقية tissue, paper towel

manadeel siHeeya مناديل صحية sanitary [pad BE] napkin

mandeel lil-maa'ida منديل للمائدة napkin

maneekoor منيكور manicure

mantaqa منطقة region

mantaqat al-nuz-haat منطقة النزهات picnic area

mantaqat al-tasawooq منطقة التسوق shopping area

maq'ad مقعد seat

maq'ad 'alal mamsha مقعد على الممشى aisle seat

maq'ad 'alal-naafiza مقعد على النافذة window seat

maq'ad sayaara مقعد سيارة car seat

maqha مقهى cafe, coffee shop

maqhan internet مقهى إنترنت internet cafe

mara مرة once

mareed مريض sick [ill BE]

mareed bil-rabu مريض بالربو asthmatic

mareed bil-sukaree مريض بالسكري diabetic

marHaban مرحبا hi

marham مرهم cream (ointment)

markaz al-a'aamaal مركز الأعمال business center

markaz al-madeena مركز المدينة downtown area

markaz al-shurta مركز الشرطة police station

markaz al-tijaaree مركز تجاري shopping mall [centre BE]

martabaan مرطبان jar

marwaHa مروحة fan (appliance)

masaa' مساء evening, night

masaa' al-khayr مساء الخير good afternoon, good evening

masaaj مساج massage

masaana مثانة bladder

masbaH مسبح pool

masbaH lil-atfaal مسبح للأطفال kiddie [paddling BE] pool

masbaH masqoof مسبح مسقوف indoor pool

mashghool مشغول busy

mashroob مشروب drink n

mashroobaat قائمة المشروبات drink menu

masmooH مسموح allowed

masraH مسرح theater

masraHeeya مسرحية play n (in theater)

masrooq مسروق stolen

mata متى when

mataar مطار airport

mat'am مطعم restaurant

matar مطر rain n

matbakh مطبخ kitchen

mat-Haf متحف museum

mawaad tanzeef مواد تنظيف cleaning supplies

mawaa'eed al-ziyaara مواعيد الزيارة visiting hours

mazaar مزار shrine

mazalla مظلة umbrella

mazra'aa مزرعة farm

meekaaneekee ميكانيكي mechanic

meekroowayif مايكرويف microwave

metro al-anfaaq مترو الأنفاق subway [underground BE]

mi'ada معدة stomach

mi'asam معصم wrist

mi'ataf معطف coat

mi'ataf lil-matar معطف للمطر raincoat

mibrad lil-azaafir مبرد للأظافر nail file

midmaar al-sibaaq مضمار السباق racetrack

midrab مضرب racket (sports)

mifsal مفصل joint (of body)

miftaH مفتاح key

miftaH al-ghurfa مفتاح الغرفة key card

miHfaza محفظة wallet

mikhadda مخدة pillow

miknasa مكنسة broom

miknasa kahraba'eeya مكنسة كهربائية vacuum cleaner

mikwa مكواة iron (for clothes)

mil'aaqa ملعقة spoon

mil'aaqa lil-'aayaar ملعقة للعيار measuring spoon

mimsaHa ممسحة mop

min من from

min fadlak من فضلك please

minfakh منفاخ air pump

minibaar ميني بار mini-bar

minshafa منشفة towel

miqass مقص scissors

miqlaah مقلاة frying pan

mirfaq مرفق elbow

mis'ad مصعد elevator [lift BE]

misfaah مصفاة colander

misht مشط comb

mitraqa مطرقة hammer

miyaah ghaazeeya مياه غازية sparkling water

miyaah ma'adaneeya مياه معدنية still water

moh'id موعد appointment

mohqif موقف parking, stop (on bus route)

mohqif al-baas موقف الباص bus stop

mohqif al-sayaraat موقف السيارات parking lot [car park BE]

mookaasaan موكاسان loafer

moos موس mousse (hair)

moos al-Hilaaqa موس الحلاقة razor

mooseeqa موسيقا music

mooseeqa al-jaaz موسيقى الجاز jazz

mooseeqa al-poop موسيقى البوب pop music

mooseeqa al-raap موسيقى الراب rap music

mooseeqa al-sha'aabeeya موسيقى شعبية folk music

mooseeqa Haya موسيقى حية live music

mooseeqa klaaseekeeya موسيقى كلاسيكية classical music

mu'aaq معاق handicapped [disabled BE]

mu'adeeya معدية ferry

mu'atamar مؤتمر conference

mubakkir مبكر early

mubtadi' مبتدىء beginner

mudadaat al-Hayaweeya مضادات حيوية antibiotics

mudakhan مدخن smoked

mudda مدة period (of time)

mudeer مدير manager

mud-hish مدهش amazing

mu'din معد contagious

mughaadara مغادرة departure

mughaadarat al-funduq مغادرة الفندق check-out (from hotel)

mughlaq مغلق closed

muHaamee محامي lawyer

muHaasaba محاسبة invoice n

muHaasib محاسب cashier

muHatta محطة station (railroad)

muHawwil محوّل adapter

muhd atfaal مهد أطفال crib [cot BE]

muHlee sinaa'ee مُحلي صناعي artificial sweetener

mu'idaat معدات equipment

mu'idaat lil-ghats معدات للغطس diving equipment

mujaffif sha'ar مجفف شعر hair dryer

mujmal مُجمل total

mujmoo'a مجموعة group

mujoharaat مجوهرات jewelry

mukaalamat eeqaaz مكالمة إيقاظ wake-up call

mukayyef al-hawaa مكيف الهواء air conditioner

mukhaalafa مخالفة fine (for breaking law)

mukhayyam مخيم campsite

mulaakama ملاكمة boxing

multahib ملتهب infected

multaqee al-turuq ملتقى الطرق intersection

multawee ملتوي sprained

mumarid ممرض nurse

mumill ممل boring

mumtaaz ممتاز super (fuel)

mumtir ممطر rainy

munaasib مناسب suitable

munaasib lil-maykrowayf مناسب للمايكروويف microwaveable

munazzif منظف detergent

munfasil منفصل separate

munHadar منحدر cliff

munHadir khaas li-kursee al-muq'aadeen منحدر خاص لكرسي المقعدين wheelchair ramp

munHafed منخفض low

munhak منهك exhausted

munqiz منقذ lifeguard

muntasif al-layl منتصف الليل midnight

muntasif al-nahaar منتصف النهار noon

muqaabil مقابل opposite

muraaqabat jawazaat al-safar مراقبة جوازات السفر passport control

murabeeyat atfaal مربية أطفال babysitter

murtaaH مرتاح well-rested

musaa'ada مساعدة help n

musaab bi-daa' alsura' مصاب بداء الصرع epileptic

musaab bi-emsaak مصاب بإمساك constipated

musaab bi-fuqr al-dam مصاب بفقر الدم anemic

musaab bi-madd al-nazar مصاب بمد النظر far- [long- BE] sighted

musaab bi-qasr al-nazar مصاب بقصر النظر near- [short- BE] sighted

musaafir مسافر passenger

musabaq al-dafa' مسبق الدفع prepaid

musabbit al-sha'aar مثبت الشعر hairspray

museer lil-ehtimaam مثير للاهتمام interesting

mushkila مشكلة problem
mushmis مشمس sunny
musinn مسن senior citizen
muslim مسلم Muslim
musr مصر Egypt
musree مصري Egyptian
musta'ajil مستعجل urgent
mustaqeem مستقيم straight
mustashaar مستشار consultant
mustashfa مستشفى hospital
muta'akhir متأخر late (time)
mutallaq مطلق divorced
mutamarras متمرس experienced
mutaqaa'id متقاعد retired
mutarjim مترجم interpreter
mutawassit متوسط medium (size)
mutazawij متزوج married
muwaqata مؤقت temporary
muzeel al-raa'iHa مزيل الرائحة deodorant
muz-hil مذهل stunning

N

naadee نادي club
naadee laylee نادي ليلي nightclub
naadee lil-raqs نادي للرقص dance club
naadee li-mooseeqa al-jaaz نادي لموسيقى الجاز jazz club
naafiza نافذة window
naafoora نافورة fountain
na'am نعم yes
nabaatee نباتي vegetarian
nadwa ندوة seminar
nafs نفس same
nahar نهر river
nazaaraat نظارات (eye)glasses
nazaaraat shamseeya نظارات شمسية sunglasses

nazarhu da'eef نظره ضعيف visually impaired
nazeef نظيف clean adj
nisf نصف half
nisf keelo نصف كيلو half-kilo
noh'eeya نوعية quality
nuHaas نحاس copper
nuskha نسخة photocopy
nuz-ha نزهة walk n
nuzul نزل hostel

O

ohqaat al-'aamal أوقات العمل office hours
ohqaat al-'aamal أوقات العمل business hours
ohtaad lil-khayma أوتاد الخيمة tent peg
'omaan عمان Oman
omaanee عماني Omani
oorkeestra أوركسترا orchestra
ootoomaateekee أوتوماتيكي automatic
ostraalee أسترالي Australian
ostraaleeya أستراليا Australia

Q

qaa'at ejtimaa'aat قاعة اجتماعات meeting room
qaa'at al-al'aab قاعة الألعاب arcade
qaa'at al-Haflaat al-mooseeqeeya قاعة الحفلات الموسيقية concert hall
qaa'at al-mu'atamaraat قاعة المؤتمرات convention hall
qaa'imat al-nabeez قائمة النبيذ wine list
qaa'imat al-ta'aam قائمة الطعام menu

qaa'imat ta'aam lil-atfaal قائمة طعام للأطفال children's menu

qaa'imat ta'aam ma' al-as'aar قائمة طعام مع الأسعار fixed-price menu

qaarib قارب boat

qaarib al-najaah قارب النجاة life boat

qabl قبل before

qadam قدم foot

qadeem قديم old

qahwa قهوة coffee

qal'a قلعة castle

qalb قلب heart

qamaama قمامة trash [rubbish BE]

qamees قميص shirt

qareeb قريب close, near

qasdeer قصدير pewter

qaseer قصير short

qasr قصر palace

qassat sha'ar قصة شعر haircut

qatar قطر Qatar

qataree قطري Qatari

qatra قطرة drop (of liquid)

qeema قيمة value n

qeeyaas قياس size

qibla يبوس kiss v

qifl قفل lock n

qimma قمة peak n

qit'aa قطعة piece

qit'aa naqdeeya قطعة نقدية coin

qitaar قطار train n

qitaar saree' قطار سريع express train

qob'aa قبعة hat

qudaas قداس mass (in church)

qudoom الوصول arrivals

qusoor feel qalb قصور في القلب heart condition

qutn قطن cotton

R

radee' رديء bad

radee'a رضيع baby

rajul رجل man

rakhees رخيص cheap

ramaadee رمادي gray

ramz al-balad رمز البلد country code

ramz al-mantaqa رمز المنطقة area code

raqaa'iq aluminyoom رقائق المنيوم aluminum [kitchen BE] foil

raqm رقم number

raqm al-faks رقم الفاكس fax number

raqm far'ee رقم فرعي extension

raqm al-siree رقم السري PIN

raqm tilifoon رقم تلفون phone number

raqs رقص dancing

ra's رأس head

raseef رصيف platform

rashH رشح cold n (illness)

rasm رسم fee

rasm al-dukhool رسم الدخول admission (to museum etc)

rasm al-khidma رسم الخدمة cover charge

rasm al-sarf رسم الصرف exchange fee

ratl رطل pound (weight)

ri'a رئة lung

ridaa'aa رضاعة baby bottle

ridfayn ردفين buttock

riHla رحلة excursion, trip

riHla bil-qaarib رحلة بالقارب boat trip

riHla johweeya رحلة جوية flight

risaala رسالة letter

risaala رسالة message

rool رول roll
roomaansee رومانسي romantic
rukba ركبة knee
rukhsa qeeyaada رخصة قيادة
  driver's license
rukoob al-daraaja ركوب الدراجة
  cycling
ruqba رقبة neck
rusoom رسوم جمركية duty (customs)

S

saa'a Haa'iteeya ساعة حائطية clock
saa'aa ساعة hour
saa'at yad ساعة يد watch n
saaboon صابون soap
saaHat al-madeena ساحة المدينة
  town square
saaHib صاحب boyfriend
saahiba صاحبة girlfriend
saa'il li-ghaseel al-suHoon سائل
  لغسيل الصحون dishwashing
  [washing-up BE] liquid
saakhin ساخن hot
saalat seenema صالة سينما movie
  theater
saaloon kuwaafeer صالون كوافير
  hair salon
saaohna ساونا sauna
saaq ساق leg
sabaaH صباح morning
sabaaH al-khayr صباح الخير good
  morning
sabee صبي boy
sabgha صبغة color
sadadaat qutneeya lil-sayidaat
  سدادات قطنية للسيدات tampon
saddee ثدي breast
sadeeq صديق friend
sadr صدر chest

sa'eed سعيد happy
saff صف class (in school)
sagheer صغير little, small
saHab min al-Hisaab سحب من
  الحساب debit
saHeeH صحيح right, correct
sahil سهل easy
saHn صحن dish, plate
saHraa' صحراء desert
sakaakir سكاكر candy [sweets BE]
sakhunat aktar min al-laazem
  ساخن أكثر من اللازم overheated
salaalim kahrabaa'eeya سلالم
  كهربائية escalator
salaat صلاة service (in church)
salb سلب mugging
saloon tajmeel صالون تجميل nail
  salon
sama'aat سماعات headphone
sam'ee da'eef سمع ضعيف hearing
  impaired
samm سم poison
sana سنة year
sandal صندل sandals
santimeter سنتمتر centimeter
sa'oodee سعودي Saudi;
  al-sa'oodeeya السعودية Saudi
  Arabia
saraaf al-aalee صراف آلي ATM
saree' سريع fast
sareer سرير bed
sareer atfaal سرير أطفال crib [cot
  BE]
sareer mufrad سرير سفرد single bed
sareer muzdowaj سرير مزدوج
  double bed
sareer qaabil lil-tawwi سرير قابل
  للطوي cot [campbed BE]
sayaaH سائح tourist

217

sayaara سيارة car

sayaara fakhma سيارة فخمة luxury car

sayaara musta'ajara سيارة مستأجرة rental [hire BE] car

sayaarat al-es'aaf سيارة الإسعاف ambulance

saydaleeya صيدلية pharmacy [chemist BE]

see dee سي دي CD

seeghaar سيجار cigar

selseeyoos سلسيوس Celsius

shaab شاب young

shaaHina qaatira شاحنة قاطرة tow truck

sha'ar شعر hair

shaare' شارع street

shaatee' شاطىء beach

shadeed al-enHedaar شديد الانحدار steep

shafaraat al-Hilaaqa شفرات الحلاقة razor blade

shahaada شهادة certificate

shahr شهر month

shajr شجرة tree

shakwa شكوى complaint

shalaal شلال waterfall

shama' khat al-beekeenee شمع خط البيكيني bikini wax

shampoo شامبو shampoo

shams شمس sun

sharaashif شراشف sheet

shareeHat شريحة slice

sharq شرق east

sheek شيك check (payment) [cheque BE]

sheek seeyaaHee شيك سياحي travelers check [traveller's cheque BE]

shibshib شبشب slipper

shiffa شفة lip

shimaal شمال north

shiqqa شقة apartment

shirkat ta'ameen شركة تأمين insurance company

shnurkel شنركل snorkeling equipment

shohka شوكة fork

shoort شورت shorts

shukran شكراً thank you

shurta الشرطة police

siHHa صحة health

sijaa'ir سجائر cigarette

sikeen سكين knife

silla سلة basket

sinn سن tooth

si'r سعر price, charge (cost)

si'r al-sarf سعر الصرف exchange rate

si'r muHaddad سعر محدد fixed-price

sirqa سرقة theft

sirwaal daakhilee سروال داخلي briefs [underpants BE]

sitrat al-najaah سترة النجاة life jacket

siwaar سوار bracelet

SMS اس ام اس text message

soht aa'ala صوت أعلى louder

sooda صودا soda

soodaanee سوداني Sudanese; al-soodaan السودان Sudan

soof صوف wool

soopermarkit سوبر ماركت supermarket

sooq سوق market

soora صورة photograph

sooree سوري Syrian

sooriyaa سوريا Syria

spa سبا spa
su'aal سعال cough *n*
su'aal سؤال question
sudaa' صداع headache
sundooq صندوق package
sundooq al-bareed صندوق البريد
  mailbox [postbox BE]
su'ub صعب difficult
suwwar dijeetaal صور دجيتال digital
  photo

T

ta'aam طعام food
ta'aam lil-rada' طعام للرضع baby
  food, formula
ta'aam mujammad طعام مجمد
  frozen food
ta'aatul تعطل breakdown
ta'abaan تعبان tired
taabe' طابع stamp *n*
taabiq al-ardee طابق أرضي ground
  floor
taa'eh تائه lost
taa'ira طائرة airplane
ta'ajeer al-sayaraat تأجير السيارات
  car rental [hire BE]
taalee تالي next
taalib طالب student
taalif تالف damaged
ta'ameen تأمين insurance
ta'areekh تاريخ date (on calendar)
ta'atal تعطل broke down
taawala طاولة table
tabaq al-yohm طبق اليوم menu of
  the day
tabaq edaafee أطباق إضافية side
  dish
tabdeel al-'umlaat تبديل العملات
  currency exchange

tabdeel taa'ira تبديل طائرة
  connection (in travel)
tabeeb طبيب doctor
tabeeb asnaan طبيب أسنان dentist
tabeeb atfaal طبيب أطفال
  pediatrician
tabeeb nisaa'ee طبيب نسائي
  gynecologist
tadfi'a تدفئة heater [heating
  BE]
tafH jildee طفح جلدي rash *n*
taHmeed تحميض develop (film)
taHweela تحويلة detour
takhdeer تخدير anesthesia
takhfeed تخفيض discount
takhreem تخريم lace
taksee تاكسي taxi
talb tohseel طلب توصيل hitchhike
talj ثلج ice
tallaaja ثلاجة refrigerator
tanoora تنورة skirt
tanzeef al-wajah تنظيف الوجه
  facial *n*
taqleedee تقليدي traditional
taqm طقم suit (clothing)
taqreer al-shurta تقرير الشرطة
  police report
taqs طقس weather
tareeq طريق road, route
tareeq aakhar طريق آخر alternate
  route
طريق للخيول
  horsetrack
tareeq bi-rasm muroor طريق برسم
  مرور toll road
tareeq saree'a طريق سريع highway
  [motorway BE]
tasawooq تسوق shopping
tashanuj تشنج cramp

tashgheel تشغيل on

tasjeel sayaara تسجيل سيارة vehicle registration

tasleeya تسلية entertainment

tasreeH jumrukee تصريح جمركي customs declaration form

tasweer bil-flash تصوير بالفلاش flash photography

tatreef sha'ar تطريف شعر trim (haircut)

tawaal al-layl طوال الليل overnight

tawaari' طوارىء emergency

tawaqoo'a al-taqs توقعات الطقس forecast

taweel طويل long

tayr طير bird

tazkara تذكرة ticket

tazkara elektroneeya تذكرة الكترونية e-ticket

tazkara lil-baas تذكرة للباص bus ticket

tazkara zehaab wa-'ohda تذكرة ذهاب و عودة round-trip [return BE] ticket

tee sheert تي شيرت T-shirt

televiziyoon تلفزيون TV

tennis تنس tennis

terminaal تيرمنال terminal (airport)

tifl طفل child

tilifoon تلفون phone *n*

till تل hill

tooaleet تواليت restroom

toonis تونس Tunisia

toonisee تونسي Tunisian

toowaaleet تواليت restroom [toilet BE]

toowaaleet khas lil- mu'aaqeen تواليت خاص للمعاقين disabled restroom [toilet BE]

toowaaleet kimiyaa'ee تواليت كيميائي chemical toilet

tughaadir تغادر leave (airplane)

turaddi' ترضّع breastfeed

turuq al-sayr طرق السير walking route

U

'uboor mushah عبور مشاة pedestrian crosswalk [crossing BE]

ujra idaafeeya أجرة إضافية surcharge

ukht أخت sister

'ulba علبة box

'umla عملة currency

umm أم mother

'umr عمر age

'unwaan عنوان address

'unwaan elektroonee عنوان الكتروني e-mail address

'uqd عقد necklace

urdunnee أردني Jordanian; **al-urdun** الأردن Jordan

usboo' أسبوع week

usboo'ee أسبوعي weekly

'utlat nihaayat al-'usboo' عطلة نهاية الأسبوع weekend

'utr عطر perfume

'utr ba'ad al-Halaaqa عطر بعد الحلاقة aftershave

uzn أذن ear

V

van فان van

W

waadee وادي valley

waadiH واضح clear *adj*

220

waaHid واحد one

waaqee shamsee واقي شمسي sunblock

waaqee zikree واقي ذكري condom

waasia' واسع loose (fit)

waHdee وحدي on my own

wajabaat asghar lil-atfaal وجبات أصغر للأطفال children's portion

wajah وجه face

wajba وجبة meal

wakaala وكالة agency

walaa'a ولاعة lighter (cigarettes)

waqt وقت time

warq ورق paper

warq toowaaleet ورق تواليت toilet paper

wasfa tibeeya وصفة طبية prescription

wazn amti'a zaa'id وزن أمتعة زائد excess luggage

wi'aa' lil-tabkh وعاء للطبخ pot

wisikh وسخ dirty

Y

ya'akhuz يأخذ take v

ya'akul يأكل eat

ya'amal يعمل work v

ya'anee يعني mean v

yaaqa mudawwara ياقة مدورة crew neck

ya'atee يأتي come

yab'as SMS يبعث اس ام اس text v

yabda' يبدأ begin, start v

yabee'a يبيع sell

yabtala'a يبتلع swallow v

yad يد hand

yadfa' يدفع pay v

yadfa' يدفع push v

yadkhil يدخل insert v

yadkhul يدخل enter

yadkhul 'alal internet يدخل على الإنترنت log on

yadkhul feel-sayr يدخل في السير merge

yadrus يدرس study v

ya'eesh يعيش live v

yafham يفهم understand

yafHas يفحص check v

yafqud يفقد lose (something)

yaftaH يفتح open v

yaghliq يغلق close v

yaghtus يغطس dive v

yaHjuz يحجز reserve v

yaHsal يحصل happen

yajid يجد reach (person)

yajlib يجلب bring

yajlis يجلس sit

yakhlaa' يخلع extract v (tooth)

yakhruj يخرج exit v

yakhruj min al-internet يخرج من الإنترنت log off

yakoon يكون be

yal'ab يلعب play v

yaltaqee يلتقي meet v

yamanee يمني Yemeni; **al-yaman** اليمن Yemen

yameen يمين right (direction)

yamHi يمحي delete v

yansaH ينصح recommend

yantahee ينتهي end v

yantazar ينتظر wait v

yanzif ينزف bleed

yanzil ينزل get off (a train/bus/subway)

yanzil ينزل descend, stay v

ya'ood يعود return v

yaqbal يقبل accept

yaqees يقيس fit v (clothing)

yaqful يقفل lock up
yaqif يقف stop
yaqood يقود drive v
yaqta' al-ettisaal يقطع الاتصال disconnect
yaquss يقص cut v (hair)
yarqus يرقص dance v
yasaar يسار left (direction)
yasaff يصف park v (car)
yasbaH يسبح swim v
yash'aal يشعل light v (cigarette)
yas-Hab يسحب withdraw, pull
yash'al يشعل turn on (light)
yash-Han يشحن recharge v
yashmal يشمل include
yashoof يشوف look v
yashoof يشوف see
yashrab يشرب drink v
yashtaree يشتري buy v
yash'ur bi-duwaar يشعر بدوار dizzy
yash'ur bi-ghasayaan يشعر بغثيان nauseous
yasil يصل arrive
yasriq يسرق steal
yasta'ajir يستأجر rent v [hire BE]
yastakhdim يستخدم use v
yastamata' يستمتع enjoy
yastaqbil يستقبل receive v
yata'akhar يتأخر delay n
yatakallam يتكلم speak
yatanaffas يتنفس breath
yataqaya' يتقيأ vomiting
yatasaaqat al-talj يتساقط الثلج snowy
yatazawaq يتذوق taste v
yatba' يطبع print v
yatbukh يطبخ cook v
yat'fa' يطفئ turn off (light)
yatlub يطلب charge v, order

yatruk يترك leave v (deposit)
yattasil يتصل call (telephone)
yattasil يتصل contact v, connect, phone
yattasil laaHiqan يتصل لاحقاً call back
yaz-hab يذهب go
yazoor يزور visit v
yidghut يضغط dial v
yikbis يكبس press v (clothes)
yikhla' يخلع take off (shoes)
yimla يملأ fill out (form)
yimla يملأ fill up (tank)
yohm يوم day
yohqiz يوقظ wake (person)
yu'atee يعطي give
yu'aanee min al-Hasaaseeya يعاني من الحساسية allergic
yu'aaniq يعانق hug v
yu'addel يعدل alter
yu'akid يؤكد confirm
yu'alim يؤلم hurt v
yu'asar feel ghasaala يعصر في الغسالة tumble dry
yubaddil يبدل change (money); exchange v; transfer
yuballigh 'an يبلغ عن report v
yughaadir يغادر leave (go away)
yughassal يغسل wash v
yughayer يغير change v
yuHibb يحب like, love v (someone)
yujad jeleed يوجد جليد icy
yukalif يكلف cost v
yukassir يكسر break (tooth, bone)
yukhayem يخيم camp v
yukhbir يخبر notify
yuktub يكتب write (down)
yunqush ينقش engrave

yuqaddim يقدم introduce
yuraafiq يرافق accompany
yuraqi'a يرقع patch
yuree يري show v
yursil يرسل send
yusakhin يسخن warm v
yusalliH يصلح repair v
yushir يشير point v
yutarjim يترجم translate
yut'im يطعم feed v (baby)
yuwaqe'a يوقع sign v

Z

zaa'ida al-doodeeya زائدة دودية
  appendix
zaalik ذلك that
zaaweeya زاوية corner
zahab ذهب gold
zahab abyad ذهب أبيض white gold
zahab asfar ذهب أصفر yellow gold
zahra زهرة flower

zahree زهري pink
zala'a ضلع rib
zameel زميل colleague
zarf ظرف envelope
zayit زيت oil
zehaab ذهاب one-way [single BE]
  (ticket)
zehaab wa-ohda ذهاب وعودة
  round-trip [return n BE] (ticket)
zibdah زبدة butter
zifr ظفر fingernail
zifr esba' al-qadam ظفر إصبع القدم
  toenail
ziraa' ذراع arm
zohj زوج husband
zohja زوجة wife
zohraq زورق motorboat
zubdeeya زبدية bowl
zuhr ظهر back (of body)
zujaaj زجاج glass (material)
zujaaja زجاجة bottle